RAISE YOUR HAND

MARKETING

How to consistently & predictably buy
life time customers

Joshua Bardsley & Bradley J Sugars

CONTENTS

PART 1

PART 2

PART 3

Foreword

This book is going to walk you through marketing in a way you may not have thought about. We all know marketing is, unfortunately, one of the first things that gets turned off during a crisis or downturn. This is quite simply like turning the tap off and still expecting the bath to fill up with new customers and get you out of your rut - it's not logically correct. I constantly hear that marketing is deemed as a cost and this is nearly always due to a lack of clarity about what is working and what isn't. When I owned my dog food business, I asked a radio advertiser which ads were performing the best. She said 'Oh, you don't know which half of your marketing actually works'. As an accountant, my head almost rolled off and I knew that people were throwing money at the wall to hope it would stick. In order to be clear and comfortable with any expense, we need to know the benefit we receive from it so the name needs to be with our marketing investments. By adding something called a conversation rate and focusing our marketing on the simple interaction of talking with prospects, we can create clarity on our numbers and begin to build some comfort into our marketing investments. This book will talk you through why conversational marketing is a revolutionary method of adding consistency, predictability, and profitability to your marketing, as well as removing all concern whether your marketing is working or not.

RAISE YOUR HAND MARKETING

Learning is the most important part of any business owner, executive, or entrepreneur's life. A great man by the name of Jim Rohn once told me that 'once you out-learn me, you can out-earn me'. I took that very literally and have read over 2,800 books since. When I first met Josh in 2014, he was a kid full of energy who wanted to know how to become 'successful'. I told him the same thing, and he went on to read hundreds of books, including all of mine in about 3 weeks, which has eventually led to us building great businesses and writing this book. You have everything you ever wanted to come but now it's training time, training to become an investor rather than a manager. An investor seeks to compound their growth and will repeat things until they are near perfection. Repetition feels rough and learning can be boring, but you are sowing seeds that will allow you to deal with future problems and challenges.

Time is an asset we discuss a lot in this book. Money is often the currency of marketing, with all the talk of budgets and profits, and time takes the back seat. Using time as a measurable investment tool, due to it usually carrying a cost, is an important realization that will enable you to plan effectively and budget properly. On nearly every occasion where I have looked at a plan or been in a marketing discussion, time investment and the cost attached to it is largely ignored. How much time are you paying for in your business at the moment that is not being fully utilized? This is a great question to think about. All time available should be used for conversation or service development. If you want to achieve your goals quicker, by thinking about how much you are going to proactively spend on each marketing strategy and adding thoughts about how you can re-leverage your current time, your team's time and platforms that utilize time as the key spend will enable you to be a more effective planner. Understanding your overall goals will help you work backwards to the number of conversations required to achieve it. That number is out there now and there is a plan that can be built to achieve it, as quick as you want it should you have the required human and financial capital. Get yourself excited but be smart. Getting a true picture of the time available will help you with the processes we outline for the execution of a well-run marketing plan. You need to know these things. Plans are nearly always developed first before looking clearly at the operational capacity and the issues that can be created through scaling up.

FOREWORD

'People overestimate what they can do in one year but underestimate what they can do in 10' is a great quote that puts the previous paragraph into perspective. Conversations are predictable and consistent with the right strategies and will help you see control in your growth. The trick is not to overdo it. Be patient, be calculating and know your numbers as well as a delivery capacity that maintains exceptionally high quality of product or service.

This is not a story book; it's a manual. Re-read the chapters and write notes on how the theory fits your industry and goals. The first part will take you through various examples and practices that should align your mindset and help you become a farmer of relationships. It has repetition and it goes over theories in different ways. This has been done to build consistency of language for you so that by the time you reach the planning and strategy phases, you are thinking in the right way. It takes practice and we want you to come back to whatever segment or chapter is required for the current challenge you are facing. Some of you have been marketing for a long time and the theory in this book will be different to your current way of working. Go into reading it with an open mind and get ready to begin enjoying your growth.

Whilst some of the stories and sections of this book may not be relevant to your industry exactly, read them. Stories and examples are phenomenal ways to get ideas flowing.

P.s if you see small comments as you work through the book in italic, that is personal comments on the subject being discussed, more than likely a story or two.

Breakdown

Here is a breakdown of the parts of the book

Part 1 - Theory

A new chef will spend hours repeating and learning processes, often spending countless numbers of those hours doing simple tasks like chopping onions or peeling potatoes. This repetition for our older readers is 'wax on, wax off'... Warren Buffett once said that 'The chains of habit are too light to be felt until they are too heavy to be broken'. As a business person it's often lonely and the learning you do on a daily basis is massively long-term. A good chunk of this book is going to be an attempt to turn you from a hunter to a farmer. A farmer sows seeds, spends 6 months waiting and then begins a harvest which will lead to consistency after the initial time investment. A hunter is a hero. He waits in the wings and gets a catch every now and again; he can't plan it. You are going to rinse and repeat, learn the process and then start taking some action.

BREAKDOWN

Part 2 - Execution

A dive into building a strategy, starting with your target, offer and copy, followed by various platform ideas and then execution. We will give you lots of ideas and examples to create a plan that enables you to roll out your new ideas tomorrow. Focus hard on the Target, Offer & Copy.

Part 3 - Conversation Development

Measurement, sales and the art of nurturing prospects to become lifetime customers.. You are here to sell and to BUY LIFETIME CUSTOMERS. In order to achieve predictable conversations, a focus on relationship development, need-finding and consistently good execution of your product or service will help you get there.

I am a coach, therefore it's my job to ask you questions, make you think, and make you run laps. You are going to run laps. In order to run laps and not give in, you need a clear reason, some pain to help you grit your teeth, and a drive to make it happen. I want you to really think about what you would like to get out of this journey we are about to go on.

Time is an asset we discuss a lot in this book. Money is often the currency of marketing, with all the talk of budgets and profits, and time takes the back seat. Using time as a measurable investment tool, due to it usually carrying a cost, is an important realization that will enable you to plan effectively and budget properly. On nearly every occasion where I have looked at a plan or been in a marketing discussion, time investment and the cost attached to it is largely ignored. How much time are you paying for in your business at the moment that is not being fully utilized? This is a great question to think about. All time available should be used for conversation or service development. If you want to achieve your goals quicker, by thinking about how much you are going to proactively spend on each marketing strategy and adding thoughts about how you can re-leverage your current time, your team's time and platforms that utilize time as the key spend will enable you to be a more effective planner. Understanding your overall goals will help you work backwards to the number of conversations required to achieve it. That number is out there now and there is a plan that can be built to achieve it, as quick as you want it should you have the required human and financial capital. Get yourself excited but be smart. Getting a true picture of the time available will help you with the processes we outline for the execution of a well-run marketing plan. You need to know these things. Plans are nearly always developed first before looking clearly at the operational capacity and the issues that can be created through scaling up.

'People overestimate what they can do in one year but underestimate what they can do in 10' is a great quote that puts the previous paragraph into perspective. Conversations are predictable and consistent with the right strategies and will help you see control in your growth. The trick is not to overdo it. Be patient, be calculating and know your numbers as well as a delivery capacity that maintains exceptionally high quality of product or service.

This is not a story book; it's a manual. Re-read the chapters and write notes on how the theory fits your industry and goals. The first part will take you through various examples and practices that should align your mindset and help you become a farmer of relationships. It has repetition and it goes over theories in different ways. This has been done to build consistency of language for you so that by the time you reach the planning and strategy phases, you are thinking in the right way. It takes practice and we want you to come back to whatever segment or chapter is required for the current challenge you are facing. Some of you have been marketing for a long time and the theory in this book will be different to your current way of working. Go into reading it with an open mind and get ready to begin enjoying your growth.

Whilst some of the stories and sections of this book may not be relevant to your industry exactly, read them. Stories and examples are phenomenal ways to get ideas flowing.

PART 1
THEORY

1

What is 'Raise Your Hand' Marketing?

I'd like to start with a story …

A young, handsome, 20-something-year-old man walks into a bar and sees a pretty girl laughing. He thinks to himself, I should go meet her. So he does.
He walks over and gets straight to the point.

"Hi, I'm Ben and I think you look amazing and you seem to have a great smile and your laugh tells me you have a great sense of humor. I think we should get married, have 2 kids and live in the country."

She looks stunned, has no idea what to say and basically just says "NO" …

This, my friend, is most marketing today. It's so blunt, so straight to the point and so embarrassingly bad that you have to call it out.

On the other hand you have a theory, a theory that if you just ask people to "Raise their Hand" you will have so many more conversations, and get so many more sales and lifetime customers that you just cannot afford to ignore it.

So Ben, next time at the bar ... maybe simply ask ...

"Excuse me, may I ask what your favorite cocktail is ...?"

Once you have the answer, go to the bar. Buy it, have it sent over and wave ...

So, let's forget Ben for a moment and get to what you are here for.

Raise Your Hand marketing is a simple tool that can be woven into every platform your marketing plan wishes to utilize. This methodology will allow you to create more human to human conversations, far more online and social media engagement, and ultimately win so much more business. A conversation is defined as two way communication. This can be digital or physical. Either one needs to be the goal of any overall strategy.

Raise Your Hand Marketing is the theory of asking your prospects to identify themselves as being interested in receiving further value from you, using every post, every email, every advertisement to get prospects to simply raise their hand...

Giving before you get is a vital mindset to have and will show itself throughout this book. This stems from the problem most businesses you come across face. Their marketing is very sales driven, meaning they ask their prospects to trust and engage with them in a transaction before the trust is earned. This is a key reason why most marketing doesn't work or creates disappointment. The phrase, 'don't get married on the first date' as an example and this should help you understand what we mean (or just think of Ben).

Any marketing strategy should be developed with trust in mind. As you are buying customers, and hopefully lifetime customers, creating a trusting environment early is key to making sure the nurturing process is as smooth as possible. Raising hands for a conversation through massive value and solution oriented campaigns will create trust-building opportunities. Care, consistency and quality will carry this through beyond your customers' initial engagement with you and create a foundation for a lifetime relationship built on delight rather than remorse.

Whilst marketing is always used to create sales and profit opportunities, most businesses burn a lot of their opportunities because they aren't nurturing properly and are too focused on the sale, which ironically will end up creating fewer sales than if they were to focus on nurturing their prospects at scale. Raise Your Hand Marketing will turn your marketing plan into a conversation and engagement machine. It will help you communicate with far more of your target market than you have in the past. This added communication, and a nurturing, trust-building mindset, will help you create a large pipeline that will be ever building strength and resilience, creating a long-lasting opportunity for success. By understanding that conversations are the initial goal of your marketing plan and making sure that all of the strategies you build out are focused on this as the 'success' outcome, you can create tools that build the trust you need for a flourishing relationship. In turn, this will develop the people in your pipeline towards the sale in a way that creates lifetime relationship opportunities. Lifetime customers are what makes your business profitable and valuable. You want lifetime customers, not single-transaction customers. You want your customers to feel you are their brand. They chose you, so your offer, copy and execution of conversation needs to reflect this. It is about them, not you.

The idea of 'raising hands' came into thought by thinking back about school. When the teacher asked a question, you raised your hand and identified yourself, taking the initiative and owning the room. This simple back and forth made you feel more engaged in the lesson and is why teachers use it. It is why so many people use conversations on stage with their audiences, and why so many brands capture your attention with conversations in movies for example, that relate to life experiences in order to make you feel that what they are discussing in some way is about you and not them. Engagement, conscious and unconscious, makes people more in tune with what it is you are saying. If your marketing copy at the moment is purely informational and about you, how can you expect your target market to be in tune with your message? By adding questions and hand-raising opportunities throughout every step of the nurturing journey, you create engagement and commitment to the message that is being said. Allow people to feel that they are choosing to engage; it is incredibly powerful.

Take a law firm, for example. This business is known for its high referral strategies and long-term business relationships feeding the client pipeline. If the law firm wanted to instead develop some outbound marketing, they would use their expertise to develop some sort of value for their prospects to raise their hands too. The law firm could develop a lead magnet that solves an imminent question or problem their client base is facing. A law firm I worked with chose a document on '10 Things Every Executive In Montreal Needs To Know About Employment Law'. When presented with this solution, a % of people will raise their hands and provide their information for further contact. Then this person, when marketed to or a conversation is requested, will have a much higher chance of engaging with the firm due to the value they have received. The prospect here identified themselves as interested in the document, creating control, and the further communication was about them and their needs.

Another example could be if you were marketing a bakery and like most, your social media posting consistent pictures of cakes, pastries and offers, you may get some engagement due to their visual and obvious dopamine-inducing nature. However, by getting your customers involved in polls, which cake looks best, ideas, and offer comparisons. For example, you can move them forward towards a hand raise, which could be 'Would you like a free chocolate eclair next time you pop by? Just DM us Eclair, or type the word Eclair below, and we will add you to the list'. By creating this identification, this one-to-one communication you now have with the prospect allows for a conversion, albeit a digital one, where you could then ask questions.

A response to the DM could be, 'Thanks for applying, I have added you to the list. Would you mind answering a couple of questions for me? I've been authorized to increase the offer to a box of 3 eclairs if you were happy to partake'. A percentage won't respond but some will and you can begin asking questions such as 'what is your favorite pastry?' 'When is your birthday?' or 'Do you have children?'. Write their name down and ask them when they would like to come in. Even if they don't give a specific time, when they do eventually come by for their box of eclairs and you know they have children, for example, you can put a couple of extra treats in for the kids. You now have a very happy shopper who will more than likely purchase something, return because of how you treated them, and of course, tell their friends about it.

The above turned a simple freemium offer into a lifetime customer opportunity and created a relationship opportunity through simple questions and conversation. This takes more work than traditional marketing because we have flipped communication on its head.

Traditional marketing = Educate (via information, as we don't yet know what our prospects' needs are) then raise hands (solving a problem based on a need).

This methodology seeks to find needs attached to what it is you sell before a relationship is formed. The results are often very small due to the percentage of people in your target market ready to buy being a lot smaller than those who may not be thinking about it at that moment.

Raise Your Hand Marketing = Raise hands (solve a problem based on a need) then educate (now via information that relates directly to their needs in order to build a relationship).

This flip means you are developing hand raising offers to generate a conversation, finding out the need and educating/solving that need. With your expertise, creating a list of imminent needs and solutions for your market as a whole should be quite easy. Due to solutions being provided for imminent problems, the customer raises their hand and chooses to engage on your offer, even if it is small. Problems facing your market as a whole are often a lot larger than the single problem your product/ service provides a solution for. It is this that will create a much larger opportunity

5

for hands raised. You are dealing with a bigger audience and an offer that people actually need, so it's obvious that more hands will be raised. It's from this conversation that leads will be generated.

Raise hands first, then educate through conversation and develop a buying relationship. More problems = more solutions = more trust = longer relationships = higher profits.

Now the previous bakery example may seem relatively simple, but the theory remains the same for any type of business and any size. A lot of books are easily applicable to business-to-consumer brands due to the volume of activity and engagement/high transactional rates, this makes examples and ideas easy and exciting. For a business-to-business company, the only reason marketing seems less exciting and less applicable for most is due to the wrong starting measurement. You measure lead flow, which is a few steps after getting a prospect to raise their hand and identify themselves as interested in what you are offering. By measuring general conversations or 'hand raises' with your target market, you can make a business-to-business marketing plan just as exciting and feel more transactional. As you get good at nurturing prospects and consistently developing trust, this will create huge opportunities for you to grow your business in a controlled, predictable way.

Raise Your Hand marketing should allow you, in time, to predictably and consistently generate prospects and nurture your relationships into leads for your business, which will in turn enable you to predict and consistently buy the number of new customers that your revenue goals demand. Growth is stressful and by being able to accurately predict and forecast conversation flow, this removes a lot of the uncertainty that comes with the day-to-day management of a growing enterprise, leaving you to focus on building trust and incorporating higher quality into your delivery and management of the business.

As well as the buying of new customers, using Raise Your Hand strategies to nurture your existing customers and consistently increase the number of transactions and average transaction value of each customer per year will ensure you are buying repeat or lifetime customers.

Three repeating areas of Raise Your Hand Marketing are predictability, consistency and sustainability. No more see-saw effect of find some work, do some work, find some work, repeat. We want you to think ahead, know where you are going and how you are going to get there. We want you to have the mentality of 'If I just deliver like I said I would, I will be successful and achieve the level of growth planned.' In order to build this mentality, you need to feel certain that the number of conversations you are having with potential customers is more than enough to convert into lifetime customers. More than you need; that is the overarching goal. Wax on, wax off!

You will achieve this through focusing on your target, offer, and copy, not the platform. The platforms will not change. You can't physically change the Google platform or the LinkedIn platform, for example. You can, however, change your target, your offer, and your copy so that it solves a problem now. By combining your target, offer, and copy with a chosen platform and key delivery process, either time or money, this creates the overall strategy that is measurable by the conversation rate. Obviously, this is marketing basics, the idea that a target, offer, and a copy make up a big element of a marketing strategy. Your offer is where Raise Your Hand takes hold and you are taught to develop offers that are far wider reaching for your audience in terms of problems solved. Most of your results will come from re-thinking your offers to be solutions to problems related to your audience, not your product. This is where the differential comes in when looking at any marketing tactics. Tweaks then to how you present the newly formed offers in a way that promotes easy engagement and delivery of said offer in return for either a digital or physical conversation can be where the magic truly begins.

Once you have an offer working and a platform you understand, compounding your process and the overall size of your plan to allow you to do so is easy. In a lot of marketing strategies and typical marketing education, the bigger you go, the worse the results get. Through case studies, we will show you that with a well thought out offer and conversation rate that is clearly determined, a diminishing rate of success doesn't need to be the case.

Check out the diagram below. Your need finding (target, offer & copy), distribution platform and process added together are what make up a marketing strategy. LinkedIn or Facebook are not marketing strategies; they are just distribution platforms. The reason we break it down this way is to make sure that each element can be focused on in a clear, tweakable way. There are at least five key measurement points broken down across the three categories that make up a strategy. The clearer your measurement points, the easier it is to see where improvements can be made and the more aware you become of what is working and what can be improved. Another reason is it makes this book easier to read and easier to return to. If the theory is where you are struggling, head to part one. If you are struggling with building your offer, head to that part, etc.

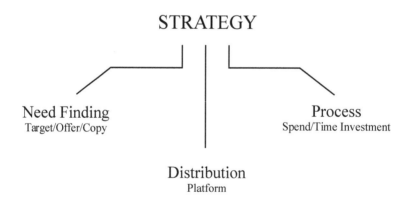

STRATEGY

Need Finding
Target/Offer/Copy

Process
Spend/Time Investment

Distribution
Platform

To put this strategy definition into context, let's look at a few examples.

Say you have an advertisement on the radio offering a free consultation with your interior design firm in London. You spend around $500 per month on this ad. The need finding element is your offer of a free consultation in London, as well as the copy of the ad that is played on the radio. The platform is the radio and the process is your investment of $500 per month. People would call this a radio strategy and get frustrated more so with the platform than the need finding or process. It's key to understand that you can't change the radio, you can change your target, offer and copy or your process.

Another example would be the telemarketing team at your consultancy practice. You give them a script to offer a strategy meeting on finance for those who are interested and ask them to call 100 people a week. The offer or 'need finding' is focused at this point on those who may have a finance issue and you are calling a large number of people to hunt for those individual cases. The platform is the telemarketing and the process is the time investment required to call 100 people. Again, you cannot change telemarketing as a platform and with Raise Your Hand theory, the 1-2% conversation rate you may achieve from 100 calls can be turned into 10-15% relatively easily by tweaking your need finding process.

The above 'strategies' haven't been maximized to their full potential by using the Raise Your Hand offer building rules, something you are going to learn later in this book but likely they will have a basic conversation rate. The key thing to understand is that your platform is not a strategy, it is only when it is added to a need and process that it becomes a strategy, giving you two tweakable areas to maximize success.

A good exercise at this stage would be to write down your current marketing strategies in the above format. Try to understand where mistakes have been made in the past in regards to you focusing more on the platform than your offer or process. If you have a conversation rate with even the most direct offers, you can actually achieve your goals with a much larger process. It's just math.

However, if you have to do 500 calls at 2% to generate 10 conversations if that's your goal, would it not be more sensible to develop an offer that has a 10% conversation rate? You then have to do 1/5th of the work finding prospects and can invest that time or money into nurturing the relationships with the 10. This is the shift you will be hearing about in the coming chapters, the move from hunting to farming, from finding to managing…

As this book develops you will learn how to execute these three areas. From now on, when you see the word 'strategy', think about those three as a whole.

2

The Ladder of Loyalty

Let's take a look at the 'Ladder of Loyalty'. This is the simple process that all of your customers go through, and was introduced decades ago when I wrote about the ladder and the theory behind creating raving fans. Before we dive into the practical elements of the book and build out your 'strategies' as per chapter 2, it's important to understand where people are on their relationship journey with you. This does a few things. Firstly, you will understand the difference between the first three rungs of the ladder and what a suspect, prospect and shopper (lead) are as well as their differences. Throughout this book, nearly all of the work is focused on turning suspects into prospects, then into shoppers. Your 'conversation rate' is typically the % conversion rate between your suspects and prospects. That doesn't mean at the beginning you shouldn't learn about what comes after someone becomes a customer. Your journey is just starting here, so embrace it and carry your trust building on for as long as the relationship lasts.

A raving fan, as you will see, is the pinnacle of your customer relationship. They are a person who loves your business and will shout about you to their friends. They are worth a fortune to you and should be the ultimate goal for all of your customers. When they are suspects and prospects, they are simply being introduced to your brand. As they move towards shopper, they are not yet customers because they have not yet entered into a transactional relationship with you over and above a single purchase. Once money and services are exchanged more than once, that is where the customer relationship begins and your nurturing process will change. This is a crucial point in the process of any business. Many companies drop the ball at this point. This singular transaction focus is very common among people because they have had that finish line in their minds since the very beginning of their journey, and as such they have become hard-wired to focus only on it. Due to the cost of acquiring a customer, most of the time it is much more difficult for a business to generate profitability on a single transaction, in some cases no profitability at all. The real profit comes from the second and subsequent transactions because the cost of buying said transaction is lower, as well as the fact that you are building a rewarding relationship that should lead to word-of-mouth referrals. The different elements to a strategy in this book are highly focused on your initial hand raise and creating a massive pipeline of prospects and shoppers. This enables you to focus on your service and the relationship rather than the hunting for new people to enter your pipeline. By removing focus on hunting for new business, it is our hope that this will provide you with the time and resources to nurture relationships further, with new customers as well as existing ones.

If you live up to shopper and customer expectations, there will be a much stronger chance that the relationship will flourish beyond the customer's first purchase. Think of the Ladder of Loyalty as a reverse funnel, with the opening to your funnel being at the bottom rung of the ladder, with it slowly inverting to a final percentage of raving fans at the very top of the ladder.

Raving Fan

Advocate

Member

Customer

Shopper

Prospect

Suspect

Suspect - When they first start out on the Ladder of Loyalty, right at the bottom rung of the ladder, people are called suspects. Our definition of a suspect is a person within the target market who has not yet had any interaction with you. Your suspect pool is the largest segment of your funnel and the biggest opportunity you have in creating massive gains for your business.

Prospect - You then move up a step to prospect. Your goal from marketing is to turn suspects into prospects and you define a prospect as someone who has taken some sort of action, like phoning in from an ad, replying to an email, sending a direct message or agreeing to further communication, like being sent something or a further call. They are not yet discussing price, they are just basic relationship opportunities. This however is your golden opportunity. You will be aiming to build a large database of prospects and continuously nurture them with Raise Your Hand marketing so that their perceived value of your organization is better than any of your competitors.

Shopper - A shopper is someone who we would define as a lead or someone who has entered into a single transaction with you. They are still shopping; they may not trust you yet and will need to be given a fantastic experience in order to come back.

Customer - To be classified as a customer, your prospect needs to have spent money or entered into a contractual relationship with you more than once. You also need to have recorded the sale in your records. As discussed in previous books I have written, this last step may seem strange and since you first introduced the Ladder of Loyalty concept in the Instant Series, technology has advanced dramatically. However, you need a clear method of differentiating between customer and prospect. Many new CRM systems have deal pipeline features where you can see your sales pipeline visually if this is preferred. Alternatively, using accounting that can easily be automated if you are a POS or ECommerce business, and equally as easily managed if you are a transactions/subscription based business. This record, though, is not just a record of payment. Your marketing does not end when someone becomes a customer; it adapts and changes. Therefore you need to make sure this differentiation is in your system so that customers who have already purchased do not receive first-transaction marketing again. Inside your customer file there should be information on where they found you, when they last bought, how often they buy, and what their average dollar sale is. I made a statement in previous books which was that I find business owners and managers put a massive stop sign at this level. The sales people seem to sit back and wait for customers to return, instead of taking proactive steps and inviting them back. That statement is the same now as it was then. However, now you really have ZERO excuses, with the amount of automation and intelligent technology available to you. Raise Your Hand marketing can and should be used, as well re-touching of customers be a part of your marketing plan. Being content with not following up with customers was scary in 2006 when the Ladder of Loyalty was introduced but now, your window of opportunity is much shorter. There is always someone lurking in the wings ready to pounce on your customers and, more philosophically, your level of comfort.

Member - You have impressed the customer enough that they are willing to give you another go. It is often during this transaction that you start to see more profitability from your customer, generally due to the acquisition cost of your marketing being a lot lower for repeat business than new business. Statistically, customers who make two purchases are nine times more likely to make more than someone who has made only one. This should be enough of a statement from me to permanently etch a repeat business 'Raise Your Hand' section into your marketing plan. By simply asking questions and furthering conversation (as well as being prepared), making sure that you are improving on previous interactions and remembering key things. Then you can ensure your client will have an exceptional experience. Remember our discussion about conversations and how you will use things our prospects need/want right now to begin conversations and then use further value gifting to generate information from the customer? This is the same as becoming a member, only deeper. Once a customer has been once, a simple strategy to have them raise their hands again will be far simpler. It is on this second transaction that you have the perfect opportunity to bring forth your membership or subscription plan.

One of my favorite methods of both improving and creating membership opportunities is asking for improvement suggestions from the customer or asking whether their service could have been better if something was added. This generally, due to ego, will have them raise their hand with suggestions. If they don't have any suggestions, I would then lean into a referral conversation and give them a value-driven offer to come back again soon as a thank you for being so positive about their experience. If they do have a suggestion, take it into consideration and make improvements. Then invite them back to try your new and improved product/service. I have seen this used on websites, in restaurants, in stores, everywhere. It goes back to the point that every customer relationship is vital and the more you converse and the customer becomes familiar with you, the easier it is for you to have a conversation with them in the long run and the more likely they are to reach out directly when they need your help.

Advocate - One of the best ways to grow your organization is and always will be referrals and word of mouth. Referral conversion rates into sales are very high and generally, the cost of referrals are very low. An Advocate, which is our penultimate rung on the Ladder of Loyalty, is a member who sells you to other people. Customers who do this are worth their weight in gold and should be treated as a capital asset. Various strategies are available for getting and keeping advocates. It simply comes down to exceptional delivery of what you do, fantastic and continuous conversations post sale, and further value offered to the prospect so that they return to the business.

Raving Fan - The top rung of the ladder is a special selection of people who cannot stop selling for you. They are often considered part of your team and most of you, if you have one, will know who you mean. They want to see you succeed, and they continue to buy from you in the long term.

Tip: If you have the resources and size, try to make sure that separate people are in charge of the different rungs on the ladder, post sale. I would have someone whose job it is to welcome first-time customers, someone whose job it is to manage members and then someone who takes care of individuals who refer your business elsewhere. This will keep clear and simple sets of KPIs available for management, simplicity again being one of the most important parts of marketing, alongside consistency.

I find the Ladder of Loyalty to be a great way to understand where a person is on their marketing journey and where each element of the funnel is in the hands of my team members. Creating engaging strategies that drive conversations and further action opportunities is part of our initial hand raising teams job and the bulk of what your marketing plan is. Prospects can be turned into shoppers more easily with conversation, and this is where a lead is generated. The definition of a lead is subject to a lot of debate. I consider a lead to be a conversation involving the exchange of money for a product/service. Generally, your sales system takes over at this point since the person is now an official lead. Some of you may have a separate team that handles this, others may be doing it all themselves. The key is to separate them and understand each stage as a different type of conversation:

Suspect to Prospect: Initial hand raise, need finding and solution development for the wider target market problems. **(Initial Hand Raising Strategies!)**

Prospect to Shopper: Secondary hand raises, nurturing through conversation to understand their need through questions. Digital or Physical. **(Sales Team)**

Shopper to Customer: Educating, matching needs to products/services you sell and relationship building through solutions. **(Sales Team)**

Customer - Member: Service, value, and trust development. **(Delivery Team)**

Your marketing is present throughout the customer's journey. At every stage of the process, problems and solutions will present themselves, as you will always be asking questions and providing value in order to move the relationship forward. One of those hand raises will be the first transaction, which is the point where the business as a whole is on stage, so to speak. Here is where you will have to prove that you are capable of delivering exceptionally well in order to create a trusting and satisfied customer who will be perfect for more marketing. Marketing at this stage, if delivery has been done well, should be a lot simpler. As above, a customer who purchases twice is nine times more likely to purchase again than someone new, so your marketing plan needs to have a major focus on this second transaction. As you will find out later on, by introducing conversation as your marketing goal and focusing on wider market needs, you will have the time to build these relationships and trust.

You learned in the previous chapter what the makeup of a marketing strategy is and will, in coming chapters, build offers to drive conversations and improve the conversation rate of the platforms you love. As you now know, most businesses are not having nearly enough conversations to achieve their goals. Conversations however, don't end with your prospects. With a conversation, you are gathering data from the outset and this data is used to personalize the experience your prospect and eventual customer, member, advocate and raving fans have with your business. If you make someone happy and provide a great, personalized service that matches their expectations or even exceeds them, you are set up for success. It pains me to think about how much business is lost through the lack of attention given to already cultivated relationships. At this point, the hardest work has been done and moving your customers through the ladder of loyalty should be an enjoyable relationship building experience where you get to show someone truly how good you are.

Survival

Survival is obviously one of the most basic human instincts and most of you won't even realize just how much of your business is run with survival in mind.

Unfortunately, with traditional marketing focusing only on those who need what it is you sell, right now, there is an entitled mentality most business owners or marketers face. They think every conversation needs to be about buying something and it is a waste of their time to have a conversation that doesn't immediately lead to this sales conversation. Do not be perturbed too much if the above mentality sounds familiar. This is a survival thought process that is instinct and will be reverted to unless you are aware and catch yourself doing it. When you are desperate and have bills to pay, you can push people to buy something before they need it or feel like it was their decision, scuppering your chances to build a solid, lifetime relationship with that customer or even have them buy from you at all. Turning yourself into a relationship manager makes sure that at every stage, accepting the next date is the prospect's decision. You can guide them with questions, experience and expertise but you cannot force it. You have to make the decision today to remove yourself from survival mode and into management mode. The prospects decide and identify themselves for the conversation. Your customers are in control and only when they need your product or service will that signal become clear. It is then your duty to ask for the sale. You know due to your target market analysis and the fact their hands were raised in acceptance of your offer that they are a prospect and therefore using questions and further fact finding to enhance their experience will make sure this signal is clear to you. You keep control whilst allowing the customer to feel like they are making the decisions. This is an important thing to understand and learn.

The questions you ask and how you deal with the answers will determine your level of success and how much further conversation is going to be required before a transaction is discussed. The switch to conversation driven marketing is going to bring big volume to the front end of your pipeline, you will have a ton of prospects. They aren't all going to be in the same position or have the need to buy right away. This is where your questions and ability to deliver exceptionally, even if there is no fee involved, comes in. Once they do buy for the first time, you need to make sure your delivery and quality is the best it can be, as if there is a high attrition rate after the sale due to it being too swift or a lack of focus being on the customers experience then your long term business prospects diminish. If customers stay once because of the lack of quality or good experience, you are fighting a losing battle and you will be constantly seeking to survive. There are three common signs of survival you should look out for. If you see one or more of these in your process, reflect on why and how it is happening, as well as how your marketing strategies can be tweaked to provide a better management pool for you to invest your time:

1. **Selling too early** - This can lead to things like buyer's remorse, which is something sales teams have to deal with on a regular basis and can be the death of a lifetime customer.

2. **Selling too late** - A trickier yet equally vital thing that is seen is when you miss a clear need and buying signal.

3. **Selling the first transaction** - Probably the most common survival instinct is to sell and then start hunting again for the next customer, leaving the person who just bought feeling like they were a cog in the machine and that they are not special. This is a very easy trap to fall for.

Do any of these sound familiar to you? Are you surviving or managing?

The Bakery

If you revisit the bakery discussed in chapter one, it's easy to see the switch from survival to management in action and how a relationship can climb up the Ladder of Loyalty. The bakery decided on their target market as families in their local neighborhood. They chose families due to the higher spend opportunity and the fact they would buy various types of product, enabling for more of a service to be offered and of course, more profitability. These families in the neighborhood at this stage are suspects, as they have not yet interacted with the business. The initial offer of a free eclair acts as a "Raise Your Hand" and asks people interested to identify themselves, meaning these people are now prospects.

When answering the questions about their family, they are still prospects. When they come in to collect their offer and have a conversation with the bakery, they receive the added value (the family extras) that was derived from their answer, the bakery has created a truly memorable experience and this will lead to a high chance of the first transaction occurring. Once the now 'shopper' makes their first purchase, as long as the bakery delivers exceptionally and through the efforts to make sure their experience is nothing like they have seen from a local bakery before, the customer will come back to purchase again. In order to stimulate a second purchase, the bakery can provide them with simple hand raises like loyalty cards and or a second purchase offers, perhaps leading to further purchases and increasing the customers loyalty to the bakery as 'their bakery'. The bakery has their customers' details and a fair bit of information on what interests them due to the conversations held, so further marketing can be more direct and focus on this information they now know is a need the customer has. As the relationship grows, more conversations are held and further transactions occur to the point where the customer may begin sharing their purchases on social media, come to events, take part in surveys and most importantly refer their friends.

Whilst the above is subjective, the simple use of conversation, need finding and constant hand raising for further engagement with the customer allows the bakery to build enough loyalty that membership programmes, referral schemes and fantastic exposure opportunities are easy to cultivate.

1

How Many Conversations Did You Have Last Week?

Now you have an understanding of where people are on their journey with you to becoming a raving fan. Here is the BIG question!

How many conversations did you have last week with prospects? Or last month? Let's take a moment to think about this and note down where they came from. Typically, you forget quickly about general conversations because these aren't sales opportunities yet, so you don't track it. This exercise needs you to look back across the last week or month to get a clear understanding of the step before you begin talking about the price. Adding tracking to this key first step is an important part of the new relationship management mindset you are switching to, as it will allow you to put tools in place to get people raising their hands at a consistent rate and build massive trust.

This is the first step to getting eyes onto whether you have been a hunter or a farmer in the past and will help you make that conscious switch to a relationship manager. Generating conversations can be far less work than it has been and we want to use that time or money saving to invest directly into our new relationships, nurturing them through the ladder of loyalty with unrivaled focus.

Take an initial snapshot of your current conversations and mark down where they came from:

Offer	Platform	No. Conversations in 2022
15% Discount	Website	5
No Offer	Referral	2

Your business may be highly transactional, it may have a long sales cycle, or it may be subscription based, for example. It doesn't matter - there is always that initial engagement or conversation, which means there is always an initial 'conversation rate' that comes from your marketing efforts. If you are an eCommerce brand where there is little human contact then how you build engagement still follows the same system.

Conversations need to be the new lifeblood of your business, whether it's a conversation you have proactively or reactively through an advertisement, whether it's a conversation on social media, email, or face to face. Measure them all, wherever they came from, and however valuable you think they are. Anywhere there is two way communication between you and someone who fits your target market criteria. No, this is not just the leads you have received, it is all interactions, so deep dive into the last couple of months and truly understand these numbers. You work with brutal honesty now, remember.

Knowing this information will help you create a base for your new plan and show you that your goals are achievable. Even if you did nothing with your target, offer or copy and just understand what your conversation rate was at current, you can make a plan for massive process growth and predictably understand what it takes to deliver that conversation goal you know will lead to the revenue numbers in your plan. Don't be alarmed if the initial number you see is low. When you measure this for the first time, conversations are often far lower than you expect and therefore it can start to become clear why your revenue may not be where you want it to be. If the level of conversations are high and your actual sales conversations are low, this is a good thing because it means that the questions you are asking and the needs you are identifying may not yet be as sharp as they could be. This is a nice place to be, as simple tweaks can create big success. Do not try to edit your numbers based on what you think they should be. This always happens when someone is asked their conversion rates when it comes to sales, for example. There is no ego required here, there is no comparison, it's just you and your business. Any two way interaction with prospects needs to be recorded, if it's a large number or small number. You cannot make the necessary changes if this number isn't right.

Most questions poised at the beginning of books are meant to trick you into thinking that you aren't doing well. In this book that isn't the case. Due to the fact that general conversation opportunities aren't measured in marketing very often, people are often shocked at just how big their funnel might be, so whatever the number you currently have, take comfort in the fact it can and will be a lot bigger. Everyone who has implemented Raise Your Hand Marketing has been able to dramatically increase the level of conversation but also improve how their relationships are managed. Don't shy away from the numbers, they speak the truth and only the truth, as long as you don't manipulate them.

A funnel, when it comes to marketing, is the diminishing volume of people spoken to as you work your way down to entering into a transactional relationship with your customer. Your marketing would start with suspects. This is the top of your funnel and is not often included in funnel diagrams because technically the suspect element of said funnel would be the size of your whole target market. Unless you plan on creating a monopoly, which is probably unlikely for anyone reading this book, doing so is more vain than practical. Whilst suspects are highly important to the planning process, having them on any form of funnel isn't practical. The new layer you will add though is prospects or conversations, something rarely included in even the most sophisticated of relationship management reports.

Why are conversations so important to Raise Your Hand Marketing?

The reason is that nearly all businesses can dramatically increase their chances of success by just engaging more and learning more about their target market. They use their potential customers' ego and remove their own. Making use of the relationship opportunities provided to you by your marketing strategies through asking questions, providing practical tools, giving gifts and being sincere will make your customers' experience with you the absolute best in class. If you use every opportunity to create more trust, need, and help, as well as show your customers that you care, there will not be a lack of opportunity for you to grow your business.

As Daniel Priestly said in his book *Oversubscribed*, you need to become famous for a very small market, not the world. Our theory fits perfectly alongside this. You don't want to become famous for the wrong reasons, so why not attempt this long lasting fame by becoming the most abundant and relationship-driven organization in your sector? Be known for how you engage, be known for how you personalize the customer's experience with you, and be known for giving. This mentality will allow you, with consistent effort, to raise hands without even trying. People will be waiting for your next products, they will be waiting for your next event, and you will have a waiting list.

Conversational marketing allows even the smallest businesses to compete in the toughest industries. Raise Your Hand allows David to beat Goliath.

A history on what marketing 'touch points' are.

Theres a lot of marketing lingo out there. Something you will hear a lot is 'touch points' and how many you might be or should be having with your prospects. A wise man once wrote a book called *Guerilla Marketing*. Guerilla warfare was made famous by the Viet Cong in the Vietnam war during the 1960s. It allowed a small force to compete with the largest, richest, and most fearsome army in the world, driving them, frankly, crazy.

Being small in business isn't a bad thing., It allows you to use strategies and tactics that larger, less nimble and agile competitors around you.

How guerilla marketing is explained by two things; touch points and consistency.

Jay Conrad Levinson, the author of *Guerilla Marketing* states that there are at least 17 touch points a prospect needs to receive before they trust a brand. Once trust is established, the advertising to that prospect/customer becomes far easier and brand fulfilling. Take the likes of Coca Cola. you trust them, you have seen their drinks in some format every day for most of our lives. Their ads now consist of non-sales approaches like their famous Christmas ad, to which a large portion of people mark as the beginning of the Christmas season. Coca Cola does not need to sell you on their drink; they have millions - if not billions - of raving fans around the world.

Now most people reading this book are not Coca Cola, nor do they have such a staple society product as their soda. You have products and services that many of your potential customers are not aware of and trust must be established as quickly as possible. The touch points discussed here equate often to conversations you have with your prospects, both digitally and physically. These are conversations that your prospect has asked for or presentation of new offers to your prospects that you have derived as a result of understanding their need from your wider market research or the answers to their questions. It all comes back to conversations and how/what you present to your client. None of Jay's 17 touches suggest selling, these are all value driven and sometimes brand driven campaigns that don't ask for anything, they just present you as the exceptional company you are.

If you think about Jay's 17 touch process and where trust is formed, it starts to make sense why most marketing campaigns do not work. In order for money to exchange, there must be a form of trust and there needs to be enough of a relationship that when the 'prospects' need matches with your product or service, they think of you. This comes from relationships and by making the switch to focusing on your market as a whole, when that market as a whole needs what you deliver, far more will be thinking about you, creating a far easier sales process.

The sheer number of organizations that attempt to enter into a transaction with only four or five touch points since the relationship was initiated is scary. They focus so much on the sale and end up damaging a huge % of their pipeline. This unfortunate yet common situation is what was discussed prior with Ben. They ask for marriage too early and will get rejected far more than they should be.

Perhaps contradicting what you were originally taught, by focusing on few instead of many, you are damaging your long-term and compounded success. Most people would rather send 100 people into their pipeline by asking for marriage and come out with 1 or 2 customers instead of carefully nurturing and farming those prospects to, in a slightly longer time period, end up with 30/40 customers from the same batch. Due to the immediate gratification of a sale, the first example here creates our short-term hero (the hunter) and for a while they are deemed the savior of the business. The farmer charges up alongside and overtakes in the long run but many businesses fail to even develop their farms in the first place.

Most of your target areas are limited at least currently, due to either distance, supply chain/operational, or time constraints. If this is the case for so many, why are you still so focused on the 1 or 2% of the market who don't need nurturing? What about the other 98%? That's your opportunity. Building strong touch points into your business and combining this with conversation is easier than you thought. Take a look at the example below from a great business who implemented this flawlessly. You will see that there were four conversations here across their typical trust building journey yet the touch points and digital communication around those conversations made sure that by the time the customer had reached the average point of sale, they had received a lot of value from the business.

This brings me to They Ask You Answer by Marcus Sheridan, where questions and concerns are thought about far earlier than they are asked about and every time a question is asked to the business, content is drafted so that this is added to the communications a prospect will receive as they go through the trust building process with the company that they are interacting with. Once you have these typical concerns or questions, its easy to build content that you can send to people in between your conversations in order to build honesty into the relationship and generate trust. Do you have the top one hundred FAQs that prospects and new customers ask of your business? It might be a good time to think about it. That way developing your own process for building trust in and around your conversations will be easy.

By bringing in conversation early, managing your touch points around your conversation with valuable, honest content and driving engagement based on the need you have found from the questions you ask, your success will be inevitable. Most of all, you will burn far less valuable prospects and create a much larger, nurturable pipeline for you and your team to manage.

Remember, a conversation is a touch point that should be purely focused on building value for the person you are interacting with. As you will find in the coming chapters, conversations are predictable and easy to generate, so you will need to develop a strong plan to nurture them before you start generating more of them.

The first mistake comes in the form of initially squeezing your marketing so that your conversations are about a sale, this leaves you with little interaction to build trust with. The second mistake comes in the form of trying to manipulate the conversation to fit your own hopeful agenda and enter into a buying relationship far too early, like a first date marriage proposal. Success comes as soon as you have the understanding that it takes a lot of trust to buy a lifetime customer and if you have learned from this chapter, your touch points are trust building opportunities.

Pulling the theory together so far:

By now, you will know how many conversations your current marketing strategies are generating and the number of conversations it typically takes in order to buy a first time customer. This number might be lower or higher than you were expecting but by having eyes on, you can predict efficiently what needs to happen, without any changes to your target, offer or copy for you to reach the revenue goals you desire. Most of you will not be happy with the conversation rate and the level of work required for you to achieve your goals. I hope that by understanding the importance of conversation and touch points, as well as seeing the power of making the switch to a relationship management focused business.

4

Hunting vs Farming

You have been introduced to the concept of making the switch from a relationship finding business to a relationship management business. This concept looks to create massive conversation flow through wide market problem solving in your offers. By going wide with your problem solving, you can ensure that a much higher number of hands will be raised and a much larger number of conversations will occur. These prospects will be earlier in their journey than you are used to but there will be high volume, meaning you can devise new tactics to nurture them, build trust and eventually create far more leads than the traditional approach.

Earlier in the book you read about hunting and farming. In both sales and marketing, there is a common phrase that says 'happy hunting', which is both hilarious and true. The definition of hunting is literally 'searching for something', so it makes sense in a marketing context with most businesses constantly on the hunt to find new people to sell too. As you read in previous chapters, the vast majority of marketers are looking for 'buyers ready to purchase' amongst their suspect pool. In most companies and within their marketing/sales departments, this mentality is what is wrong and through previous exercises you are now consciously aware of this behavior within your organization. Hunting will work, you know that but it is creating far more work than necessary.

Let's take a trip back 10,000 years ago… You are a strong hunter, with a big bow and are ready with your troup of ready hunters to go out and get the town a kill. You are a hero, you could be gone for days, you could get hurt and you could come back with nothing, but you are a hero to everyone. Your town remembers your last big kill. It was 2 years ago and everyone in the village wanted to be a hunter after that. No one has had as much success and you haven't seen a big kill opportunity since then, but they keep pushing on, in the cold, hunting away, seeking to be the next big hero. It could be a quick win, it could be tomorrow. Just the thought of it brings a sense of pride, focus, and motivation to the happy band of hunters out there in the wild.

Can you find any similarities between this 10,000 year old example and situations today?

The village nearby has had an idea to sow seeds and try to build a crop harvest, using different seeds for different seasons to bring consistency to their food sources year round, or create enough for stores through winter. It has been hard in the past and no one has had the patience to make it work. This village, though, has decided to make sure that there is around-the-clock watch and care for their crops. They know from previous attempts that it could work if the conditions are right but due to a lack of care and patience in the past, the budding crops have been left to nature and unfortunately never yielded enough for previous villages to survive on the produce, let alone thrive. The village makes a plan to nurture and water their crops day and night. The long hours and effort with no immediate gain makes the lead farmer look like a loser. The hunters are heroes, win or not. Jocks vs Nerds! After a year, the farmers' work begins to yield some produce. They have a consistent harvest and enough stores to make sure that they don't go hungry over winter. Over time, the animals in the area, due to the competing villages hunting the very few opportunities available, become scarce and the hunters become less reliable. The villages turn to the farmer and the farmer becomes the source of food. They set the price, they set the frequency, and over time, hunting becomes obsolete…

Fast forward to today, farming is one of the largest industries on earth and its patience, compounding size, and its profitability has created some of the biggest businesses in the world, meaning hunting for food has become obsolete.

Bringing this back to your business, the level of hunt-able opportunities out there and ready for the kill (sale, in this case) is low and will be getting lower each month due to the competition also targeting this very small pool. Everyone wants a quick win and that isn't going to go away. Each month there are more businesses being created, more competition for you and if you want to be successful, you have to make a change and do something differently. The farmers cultivate the whole market and eventually with enough conversations, seed sowing, and relationships, have enough business to be sustainable, predictable, and compoundable.

In nearly every industry, the number of people ready to buy now is far lower than the number of people who are not ready to buy but are prime to build a relationship with. This mentality is so common and there is a great deal of frustration within organizations' marketing departments. Almost all companies in your industry, and all of your competitors who haven't read this book, are focusing on the very small percentage. As business owners, you don't really want to get involved with a market that is overcrowded, desperate, and often price competitive. So now is the time to become a farmer and switch to high volume conversations via easy, predictable wide market problem solving and shift your and your team's time to nurturing that volume and building trusting relationships.

When you began the market research for starting your business, you probably looked into your competition, how many people there are in your target market as a whole, and made a decision based on your experience and level of talent to deliver a thriving organization within this market. Your numbers were almost certainly done with the whole of your target market in mind. You would have sliced up the market by dividing up the number of competitors around your price point, and this is what led you to make your decision to buy, start or invest. Why then, almost immediately, would you begin marketing for only the very small percentage of people ready to buy right now? You aren't the star of everyone's story and most people are not in the buying mind at all times or even aware of the fact they may need you. This is drastically reducing your actual target market and the reason why marketing is hard. You are fighting with both arms tied behind your back and whilst your processes can be upped to achieve short term goals, this cannot be consistent. By hunting you can win quickly, you can deliver volume through sheer effort but it's not sustainable. Either you will run out of people to reach out too or you will burn out. You can have the same level of conversation with 1/5th of the effort you are used to, it happens by making the simple switch from hunter to farmer.

If you focus on finding 50 people out of 1,000 that will be fast wins and four other companies are also focused on said 50 people, you will each end up with 12 or 13 customers, should all of them retain their immediate need. Although this is great, no one has given any thought to how they could engage the other 900 through a few simple steps. A common theme is "It's too much work really and everyone is very busy. Those 900 people, if they don't want to talk to me right now, are not worth my time". The truth is they do not want to talk to you about your product or service right now because they don't trust you, haven't thought about it or aren't aware. They will talk to you, if you solve a problem they have and they will do business with you when they are ready if you are the company in your industry that they trust because you helped them early on. A lot of people will buy from you quickly due to trust alone, so if you can have a conversation with lots of people and build trust early on, you will generate business both short and long term.

Statements like in the above paragraph are so common because most businesses believe that they do not have the luxury of patience and need sales now in order to stay in business. You are surviving, you read about survival in the last chapter and it's important that this point hits home. When you are simply surviving, you aren't able to focus on growth and a thriving, compounding business. What most don't realize is that they are like miners taking the scraps out of the wall who turn back just before they strike gold. You have all heard of that story before, when a miner stops a few feet away from the motherload. This is something you have seen played out in stories, books, and movies forever. Truth is, you shouldn't be in survival mode constantly, you don't need to be. Instead, your marketing should be providing you with enough conversations that YOU are limiting how many people you engage with, not chasing new customers. It is time to gain control of your pipeline and remove hope and uncertainty.

Author note: Think about it like this: for ActionCOACH, we know that only 3-4% of people that are business owners are aware that they require coaching or want coaching right now. There are 96-97% of business owners who have no interest, do not realize they could use the help or do not feel like they need the help. Our competition's marketing plans, for the most part, are all focused on 3-4% as they want sales right now and they think that their focus needs to be here in order to win quickly. They are all fighting for the now, fighting for those people who need their services instantly, and the way they portray themselves in their content and marketing strategies shows this. What it took us a while to understand was that the 96%, the huge, untapped, and zero competition percentage of our 'target market' was only a few steps behind the 3-4% that needed help right now. When we built trust with a large volume of people, new clients were signed almost as fast as if we spent five times the time hunting for those who were actively looking for what it is we do. On top of this, due to the level of conversations our coaches are now having and the fact it takes them far less time to cultivate them, it means that our team are speaking to more people than ever before and the farm is producing a predictable harvest. There had to be a mindset switch and frankly, it is still in progress but it is moving in the right direction and ActionCOACH is marketing in a far more sustainable way for our coaches and brand.

If coaches are abundant, informative, conversational, and the opposite of any-thing but helpful then they could enter into conversations with 90% of their target market with relative ease. Conversations give our coaches the opportunity to build relationships, educate and provide helpful information to people. Then, when that person faced an issue or needed help, the coach was the first person they thought of for a solution. As well as the obvious clients and new relationships, the con-versations helped us as a brand identify problems and issues that were potentially holding our prospects back in terms of their ability to achieve their goals.

Be front of mind

Farming is a method of becoming **front of mind** for your prospects. You use offers that are focused on giving value to people in order to help them know, like, and trust you. Marcus Sheridan's 'They Ask, You Answer' is phenomenal at helping you understand the concept of know, like, and trust. By focusing on creating know, like, and trust with the entire suspect pool, with value and simple single-action calls to action that allow us to have a conversation with someone to give them the value they raised their hand to. The difference between 'Raise Your Hand Marketing' and 'They Ask, You Answer' is simply that one is a fishing pole and the other is a fishing net. Both of them should work in conjunction with one another. You need to pre-answer questions across your website and blog, this will help you create know, like and trust for visitors as well as help you generate more traffic by putting your blogs in front of a wider audience. Marcus tells us that we should be thinking about wide market issues and challenges when thinking about content, which enables a wider net and brings people in. Your website, with your consistent question answering will act as that conversation tool with the website visitor and build trust with them. These trust building touch points, as you learned in the Guerilla Marketing segment of this book, will make sure that when conversation does occur with you trust is already pre-built. Raise Your Hand Marketing asks you to take this methodology and use your fishing pole to proactively search for people and ask them directly if they have the problem you can solve. If your problem is wide enough, hands will raise and in return for solving the problem you will receive a conversation opportunity for you to build trust. Combining both of these theories and putting them into practice will make sure you are being both proactive and reactive in your marketing and are building a farm that can work consistently, predictably and sustainably.

With subtle, helpful touch points that help customers solve 'now' problems, you are able to build trust without burning anyone and create longer term growth potential. Whilst not everyone will buy from you right away, the trust you are building makes sure that you will be front of mind when that prospect does need you.

Burning through potential leads is a common practice for most sales teams. It's almost as stupid as glorifying a burn rate, which is the cash we are losing on purpose to grow. To build a commercial, profitable enterprise that works without its owners, you cannot burn anything... cash or people. Your target market is probably limited in size, so anyone burnt with a marriage proposal is a no go. Don't ruin your long-term opportunities by seeking a gold strike as a hunter. You may be the hero in the short term but the farmers will catch up and take over.

This burn rate is seen as such a standard mindset, that it is portrayed in movies, tv & social media constantly. This includes investment movies such as Boiler Room, Wolf of Wall Street, or any other high paced sales environment. The hustle mentality that is shaping your social media accounts has created a mindset for most business owners that busy is good. If you aren't busy, you are losing. The truth is, the real winners are not overly busy. In fact, they are not busy at all. They have experts building systems. They are calculated and efficient. They understand their numbers and what they need to achieve daily in order to reach their desired goals. They also understand that too much activity with the wrong mindset will deliver nothing but a desolated target market and an unproductive future. The mindset you need to ensure your marketing is successful for the long term and works without you beyond your tenure as the business owner is the mindset that conversations are key and the very very simple switch to marketing to the larger, less ready, yet far less competitive market.

You are an investor. You are cultivating long-term relationships and you are investing in them. Activity for the sake of activity is the enemy to any great long-term investor.

Are you currently marketing like a hunter or a farmer?

An exercise to determine whether your current strategies are hunting or farming strategies is to figure out the type of initial conversation you are having. You should have the number of conversations you had last month to hand and therefore, be able to recall the type of conversation you were having. If you are having more conversations about price right away, the likelihood is you could be having five or six times the volume you are currently having.

Remember in the opening chapters when you learned about educating then raising hands? This is hunting. You focus on your product/service, pushing your solution out via the platforms available and wait to see who takes the bait. Sometimes you get impatient and go after the prey, making them run away. Occasionally you win but it's stressful and more often than not, you are hungry.

Raising hands via wider market solutions and then educating is farming, you are going to learn how to develop these offers in the coming chapters. You are sowing seeds on a larger scale and it becomes your job to nurture them until they are ready for harvest. Whilst this may take longer to begin with, you eventually end up with reserves of fuel that can last through hard times and you are building a sustainable future.

Let's say you are a fashion retailer. As a hunter, your ads will be discount based or you may be flurrying out flyers and handouts of offers hoping to catch a few people looking to come into the store. The problem with this is that it only works for a short while and discounting comes right out of your profit margin. Ironically, however, when things work to a small extent, you tend to see people not wanting to change. One of the most difficult things to do is change what is working, even if it is generating far less than it could be. You need to learn to be happy with constantly seeking improvement, constantly breaking systems and seeking better results.

Author note: In Avalanche we have been building Raise Your Hand campaigns for businesses for years, specifically those with a lot of locations where it is tough to get consistency of brand and results. Our campaigns typically have a 8-9% conversion rate which is very strong however in 2022, instead of being happy with this we worked hard to add platforms, touch points, and other communication strate-

gies to improve it. This change was scary to our team, they were doing fine and the resulting changes mean our delivery process now is night and day to what it was at the start of 2022. Our overall conversation rate in 2022 was 12.4% showing a 40% increase in 2021. We will likely change this further in 2023, seeking constantly to improve the number of people we can have conversations with and increase the efficiency of our clients target markets. Don't be afraid to change what is working.

If the fashion retailer above decided to adapt their strategies and became a farmer, providing the right offer and copy to solve a problem prospects may be facing on a wider scale and focus the redemption of the offer on engagement & relationship opportunities, what might happen? Let's say you are looking at women who are going on vacation this summer. Easy, right? Sure, but remember your goal is lifetime customers so it's not just about a done-and-ditch attempt to get them in to fill up their suitcase; it's about future relationship and service. You could host an exclusive evening where you invite 50 women to the store, create a small creche/nursery with an entertainer where attendees will receive gifts, provide personal attention from employees due to it being a small number of people (conversations), and create a 'stress free' environment for their vacation shopping. If marketed correctly with the problems of stress, time, childcare, and help being solved. It is almost a certainty if your targeting is correct and presented in the right way that you would have hands flinging up. Who is going to have a better chance at becoming a lifetime customer? Individuals who redeem a discount and are typically price shoppers or is it going to be those individuals who attend a wonderful event and receive exceptional service? This is just an idea and discounts can be powerful conversation starters, but don't be afraid to be bold and try new things.

There is more theory attached to this idea than meets the eye. Recall the segments of this book where you learned about understanding what your capacity is. This will lead you, based on your current conversation to customer conversion rate, to how many conversations you can have without hurting the delivery of your product or service. Most people over exaggerate how many new customers they can service without standards slipping. The fashion retailer above likely can't handle a global ad campaign bringing in thousands of discount customers and they would be far better off focusing on a smaller group of customers that will bring repeat business and likely refer their friends. The issue that a lot of people believe they are facing is that they are of the opinion their marketing needs to be huge. Most of you will not need that many conversations each month to achieve your goal, even if it is 10, 50, 100 or 500. This level of conversation can allow you to be very bespoke with your communication and deliver exceptional customer service. The instinct is to be big, fast and transactional when if you just slowed down you'd see the level of volume you need isn't that high.

Becoming a farmer isn't done overnight but you now have the tools and the numbers to determine where you are on the scale and more importantly, how your crops are doing. The ladder of loyalty is your measurement tool to understand the health of each relationship and where it needs work. You know how many conversations you can have sustainably and you have eyes on the current status of your marketing strategies. Make the switch, it will be worth the effort. You are about to learn how to begin building strategies to drive conversation growth, so make sure you have everything in the last 4 chapters clear in your mind.

5

Self-Identification

Now that you understand the difference between hunting and farming, it is time to dive into why and how prospects react to your marketing. This is one of the final pieces of the theory puzzle before you can get out in the market and start communicating. Self identification is the very start of the process that allows you to build a know, like and trust driven relationship with your prospects and eventually your customers, members, advocates and raving fans.

Self-identification is the process of allowing the prospect to choose you, raise their hand, and enter willingly into a conversation with you. This self-identification choice will lead to better trust as the prospect is in control, and if you are clever with your offer, bring in the law of reciprocity, allowing you to further your knowledge of the prospect's needs through questions.

What do we mean by 'self-identification'?

Raise Your Hand Marketing gives prospects the opportunity to identify themselves to receive the **solution** you are providing to their **problem**. You want them to raise their hands to your value proposition at each stage of their journey. This allows them to feel like they are in control and are choosing to engage with you. Control is an interesting element of the general buying process. You want to retain it whilst allowing your prospects to feel like they have it. If you can master this, relationship building and eventually selling becomes very simple. Catering for self-identification and permission in your copy brings control to the potential customer whilst you manage the narrative.

Self-identification is the act of a hand being raised via the prospect following the instructions in your copy and saying "I want this offer". In a way, all marketing asks prospects to raise their hands, just with very low levels of positive results. What you will create by allowing your prospect to retain an element of control is ownership, commitment and the removal of buyers remorse. When someone buys something they do not feel they truly chose to buy, they feel remorse which can and does lead to non-payment, cancellation or negative press with their networks. Where self-identification becomes powerful is when it is paired with a very strong, wide market offer. Typically in return for the problem being solved, you ask them for a conversation or to ask them some questions and if the copy provides control to the prospect, something called the law of reciprocity kicks in and the prospect feels obliged to communicate. The stronger the offer, the higher the level of reciprocity you will receive.

Let's say you run a wealth development business. Perhaps your service is a property investment mentorship programme. You are a leader in your field and have a high ticket product that you want the room you are presenting to to take up. Presenting an offer to a room of one hundred people may result in a few buying from you, due to their need matching exactly what it is you are selling. I have witnessed the best in the world do this and build need over a presentation with good results. While this is great, I believe that they should carry that need-building from their presentation into their hand raise offer. Instead, knowing that people in the crowd all have different levels of goals, investment capabilities, and problems they need to solve, the offer could be a one-to-one portfolio review and planning session, completely free with you or your team, as it will allow a tailored approach to their goals and the right product can be discussed if there is one that is available. You would ask the prospects in the room to identify themselves by speaking with one of your team. I am sure this would raise a lot of hands... This offers a one-to-one conversation opportunity where questions can be used to understand the prospects' needs and show them solutions you have for this problem already. Seeing as this industry is plagued with unpaid bills, drop outs and remorse from creating need rather than providing a direct solution, perhaps a change of process would be a good idea. This example would very likely see an increase in those self-identifying themselves and create far more know like and trust building opportunities in the conversation. Yes, it will take the example company a little more time but in the long run, it would be worth it.

Does this example resonate with you? When someone comes to your business for more information or engages with you online, do you seek to **create a need** around what it is you do or do you allow them to take the lead? It may be less exciting on the front end but when all is said and done, the company who listens and develops based on that will have a stronger and more reliable customer base.

As you learned previously, your conversation rate is simply the number of conversations that each strategy delivers vs the people you put the offer in front of. A good Raise Your Hand offer, focused on wider problems affecting your potential customer base and providing value in the form of a solution, should be five or six times better at producing conversations than discussions around the sale. By incorporating the theory laid out in this book, you can expect the conversation rate for even the hardest platforms to be 10 to 20%. This creates a large multiple increase in the number of conversations that you are having and relationships you are building. It also means that the workload required to achieve the number of conversations you know will drive the sales goals you desire is a lot lower, meaning more time can be spent on nurturing your relationships. This all happens by re-thinking your target, your offer, and your copy to mold it towards that self-identification, that 'I want that' feeling you create in your prospects mind. It takes more work; however, you will learn how to build relationships and educate your prospect through conversation on a much bigger scale than you are used to.

Earlier, you learned the theory of the first date. This is very simply figuring out something to do with your brand and market that your customers need right now, then allowing them to self identify as interested. This is often something small and very low cost to you that you can use as a very simple "Raise Your Hand" offering.

With Raise Your Hand Marketing, the very first step to buying profitable lifetime customers is to buy conversations. This conversation opportunity is your first date. You are giving massive value to prospects who have identified themselves and using that value to start a new relationship. The more valuable you make your offer or conversation starter, the easier it will be to develop your budding relationship into something highly profitable. Self identification at each stage, whether it be one of your touches or one of the conversations

The value and the cost of your conversation starter has to be relative to the expected acquisition cost, and of course, not reduce margins on the product or service that you do or, and often more importantly, reduce the perceived value of what you sell. In an effort to gain conversations and new customers, many brands make the mistake of devaluing the product or service by offering discounts or offering too much at this stage of customer acquisition. The conversation starter you use in Raise Your Hand Marketing should only be something that will enhance your product or service or bring awareness to who you are.

6

The Law of Reciprocity

Previous chapters have touched briefly on the law of reciprocity. In science it is defined as:

'The reciprocity principle is one of the basic laws of social psychology: It says that **in many social situations you pay back what you received from others**. In other words, if John does you a favor, you're likely to return it to him.'

Psychology plays a huge factor in any marketer's brain, as you are constantly dealing with people from all walks of life, social situations, and with different personalities. Understanding key laws and ideas around how the human brain works will allow you to be far more accurate in your planning and execution. The law of reciprocity will be your key to meaningful conversations and information you gather from them.

The mistake that is often being made is that nearly all marketing is ask-driven and the business asking gets little out of it, typically because no reciprocity is built into the exchange. If you were asked to share some of your social media posts or email marketing over the past few weeks, it is likely that you'd find they are very closed off information or an attempt to ask the prospect to do something like click a link or check out a page with little offered in return. Don't hide from this, it is very normal. It is, however, a mistake that is costing you opportunities for engagement. This same mistake is made across nearly every marketing strategy and the reason for a low conversation rate. The prospects aren't having problems solved and don't feel they owe you anything.

As you begin building a plan and putting the theory of conversation, problem solving, touch points and self identification, you will see how much reciprocity can be built. The larger the problem you solve or the larger the value you provide, the higher the level of reciprocation built and the higher the conversation rate. Your offers will be redefined to act as seeds being sown on a wide scale instead of a bow at the end of your arrow. You will become a giver and in return, you will have relationship opportunities as people will feel obliged to answer your questions in return for the offer you have given them. Your questions and ability to understand people's needs will be the determining factor of your conversation to lead %.

You are probably already thinking about what your offers could be. However, in order to execute with precision, understanding your offer budget and acquisition cost is an important first step.

You know how important it is to understand the cost of buying a new customer. How can you build an offer and develop a strong 'give' and gain reciprocity without knowing this? It becomes speculation without it and we are investors, not speculators. If you read the book *Buying Customers*, you would have learned in detail the thought process that you are indeed buying a customer. With Raise Your Hand marketing, you are taking one step back and buying the conversation. This means there will be a cost to that conversation and the higher the investment you make into the conversation, the better the conversation will be. The level of conversion rate into the customer rung of the Ladder of Loyalty will determine how much your conversation budget is. You worked this out at the very beginning of this book. Use this as your determining number for now. Yes, improvement of this number will be straightforward with more focus on building trust early and higher volume of conversation but it will give you a conservative base point for your plan.

Your marketing costs, the cost of the initial sale, and all costs associated with the purchasing of the initial transaction are called the acquisition cost. Not many people know their true acquisition cost but it is a very handy number to understand. Why? You should know at all times how much you are willing to spend to purchase a customer. This will help you understand how much you have to spend on your offers in order to buy a conversation. Once you understand this current figure, you may choose to increase or decrease it based on the profitability of the initial or lifetime value of the customer. When you add this to the conversation rate, you have the foundations to make a sensible plan. This is very basic but very often overlooked.

Most people feel uncomfortable spending money. When you dive into the true understanding of being uncomfortable, this is generally down to the unknown. When you do not know what is going to happen, the little voice in your head begins to chirp away and grow stronger as you play all of the scenarios of what could be over and over again. More often than not, the little voice sabotages you from making good decisions and can indeed lead you to make bad ones.

By understanding your numbers and becoming more focused on the lifetime value of your customers, you will begin to feel some clarity and be able to make educated decisions. You are nurturing your relationships with people so that they become lifetime customers, meaning the average number of transactions and the value of each customer should be a lot higher and can grow with effort. That means each of the investments you make has a higher opportunity attached to them and should give you more comfort in investing more into your offer and initial hand raise, where the first layers of "know, like and trust", as well as reciprocation, are built. The bigger you go in the beginning with your hand-raising offers, the greater the opportunity to purchase a lifetime customer due to the relationship created in the reciprocation. You can't do this if you don't understand your acquisition cost, profitability of initial and further transactions and then have a clear understanding of how much you are willing to spend on a customer.

Let's say you had a transaction average of $1000 and your gross profit was $400 on that transaction. Could you develop an offer that costs $200 yet solves a problem for the client and will almost certainly lead to a relationship opportunity? That level of spending may have made you feel uncomfortable but by knowing your numbers, you can see it is a sensible idea. If, on average, your customers purchased four times per year from you with no acquisition cost for the second, third, or fourth transaction, this would bring further positive reinforcement to the decision to invest more in your offer. If you knew that the relationship formed with a large investment in the prospect early would likely lead to even more trans-actions, you would feel very comfortable and perhaps want to invest even more in your relationship with them.

A good example of this would be my dog food business. We knew that each cus-tomer would spend roughly $108 with us on their first transaction. Our profit on this transaction would be $34. When checking our ads, our acquisition cost was $26 for a new customer. This meant that I was making $12 of profit on the first transaction with this customer. Through further understanding of lifetime value, I found that each customer would purchase from us 11 times, creating a total profit-ability of 1 x $12 plus 10 x $34 due to the ad not being required for the second and consequential purchases. Overall lifetime profit on a customer was $352. Based on this, I now have a much clearer budget on what I could spend to purchase a customer and I could be more aggressive with my initial offers. Back when this business was in its prime, Raise Your Hand marketing wasn't a thing. With Raise Your Hand, I could have developed a much stronger offer with the budget avail-able and reduced my cost for a conversation to a very low amount. The offer may have cost me $50 in product or value with a perceived value of $100, for example. Our business would provide a 13 point health check for every delivery on the dog, as our delivery crew were also registered veterinary nurses. Perhaps our offer could have been built around a free home health check for the prospect's dog. This would get a higher conversation rate due to it being a problem nearly all owners would be interested in and give us a perfect opportunity to have a conversation. It would cost me a little more than $26 total but I would have solved a wider problem and have far more conversations and a larger prospect base being nurtured over time.

Understanding your numbers will bring clarity to the level of offer you can put out to your market and as you now know, the larger the offer, the higher the level of reciprocity. How you build your offer and the packaging up of your target, offer and copy come next.

7

Know, Like & Trust

Raise Your Hand marketing is built with the lifetime value of your customers in mind. It may add a few extra steps, but the dramatic increase in conversations and relationships you will be building will lead to an increase in customers who are far more engaged with your brand, as long as you have the patience and actually do the work. Coupling the investment in your customers' experience and delivering your product or service exceptionally, you will not only increase your conversion rate when making a sale but also lead to a stronger overall relationship with your customer. Why does this actually happen though? It is due to the fact the customer's knowledge of you is far deeper than before, they understand what you do and they know you understand their needs fully. As well as this, due to the fact you have invested time into the relationship with them, asked them questions and tailored their experience, the customer actually quite likes you. Finally, due to the exceptional delivery and wonderful overall experience, they trust you. The work you have put in up front, unpaid and without reward was the seed that turned into a trusting relationship, a relationship that will be fruitful for a much longer period of time. You now have a lifetime customer, as long as you keep up the good work and communication.

You were introduced to the concept of know, like and trust earlier in this book and how Raise Your Hand Marketing is the proactive development of this and the likes of They Ask You Answer, by Marcus Sheridan acts as your reactive know, like and trust builder. Conversations build trust, they build awareness and time investments into the customer will create a far more enjoyable, personalized experience with you.

You are NOT too busy to invest time into your relationships and create a personalized experience for your customer. The time investment into this area of marketing will make you stand out from the crowd and create something people will shout about. This is farming, this is building reciprocity and this is development of a trusting lifetime relationship.

When you think about why you love a brand, most of the reasons can be traced back to emotional attachment, trust (formed over a long period of time via guerilla marketing techniques) or aspiration. Aspiration is an interesting one, as our trust is formed by seeing others using a product and living a 'better' life than you are. Brands and agencies know this, hence why influencer marketing is a thing. Due to the fact you have seen an influencer so many times, likely more than Jay Conrad Levinson's 17 touches, you have a subconscious trust in them. By linking a brand to this trust, the companies in question will be able to create a sort of fake trust and sell their products faster. The best companies also work on trust with you, and that's why they last. An example would be the likes of Nike, with their sports stars and high quality products but I am sure you can relate to the experience of finding a product you trusted and then did not once you actually experienced the buying process or even the product/service itself.

The concept of aspiration and emotion are going to be very important to you as you begin to develop your offers. These two key concepts are primarily found in business to consumer marketing.

Emotion: The idea of emotion in marketing is to drive on things linked to people's childhoods, collaborations with local hero businesses such as long standing consumer goods or brands. As well as this, children, family and nostalgia play a large part in creating emotional bonds. Another common theme in well run emotion driven marketing campaigns are

A phenomenal marketing campaign by Blood UK in collaboration with Cadbury's comes to mind here. Cadburys is a 100+ year old British chocolate manufacturer and has the hearts and loyalty of the country. Blood UK wanted to run a marketing campaign that would utilize this loyalty and trust customers have for the Cadbury brand to ask people to give blood. Whilst the offer was not necessarily something to buy in this case, the idea they developed had hands being raised and people self identifying by the millions. Blood UK collaborated with Cadbury's to create an advert that would see the O's, A's and B's etc removed from packaging across the country. As people saw the adverts and packaging, the trust and familiarity triggered the want to help. This highly successful campaign allowed for Blood UK to kick through the noise and head straight for their target markets' hearts.

Aspiration: Aspirational marketing campaigns are the most common theme of successful campaigns globally. This works by leaning on what you want in life and offering people solutions to these aspirations in a way they would not usually have access to. If you are a brand that wants to develop a relationship with someone, by creating an offer that gives someone something at a cost they would deem as unbelievable or access to something they did not feel they currently have the means/clout to do such as trips, events or gifts will have hands being raised at a very high rate.

Aspiration is used by millions of brands globally and is why things like outlet villages are so successful. Bicester outlet village in the UK is in the top 10 most visited public places in the country and people from all over the world fly to shop there. Why? It gives the customer access to luxury goods at a rate that is usually out of their reach normally. What happens when they buy something? The customer wears it, loves it and talks about it, allowing for indirect reach for the brand when anyone comes into contact with that customer. The goods are often items that went unsold and would usually be thrown away and in fact, the brands are accessing people that have the aspiration to be seen in that brand. This could be made even stronger by providing the customer with strong questions, ongoing customer service and touching base with them with further aspirational offers. By making someone feel special, when they have the means or trust you enough to love you, they will be a customer for life.

By providing support or solutions to someone's emotional attachments or aspirations in life, in the form of your offers, you can be sure that there will be a phenomenal level of hands being raised. What does hands being raised lead to? Conversation and personalization. Conversation leads to trust and trust leads to a valuable relationship. It is as simple as that.

As a business to business organization, you will want to focus more on ego and exposure. These two items are very easy to drive into your offers as a b2b company and will again allow you to create conversions that drive know, like and trust.

Ego: Nearly all business owners have ego, in fact, all people have ego and you do too. Everyone loves their ego being stroked so leveraging ego in marketing offers and your copy can have a dramatic effect on the success of campaigns. Business to business marketing needs to be relationship focused, therefore you need to be having conversations with as many people as possible.

A great example of ego being used in marketing is the use of interview series or collaborative content. You invite someone who is an expert to comment or discuss with you about a subject, creating content for your business at the same time. Due to using that person's expertise, this strokes their ego and will nearly always lead to a lengthy and moldable conversation. You will learn more about collaborative content later on, it is a very powerful tool that you can use to kill two birds with one stone, conversation and content.

Exposure: Why would you lean on exposure? Well nearly all businesses want to grow. Some don't, but they are a minority. Offering exposure opportunities to businesses where they are likely to be seen by potential customers for themselves is often a no brainer raise your hand for them. The best example of this is a company that threw events at their locations often and invited suppliers and potential suppliers to have a stand at the events free of charge. The suppliers were very grateful for this opportunity and nearly 100% of people said yes and raised their hand. As well as this, the conversations after the event led to nearly 70% of the suppliers doing business with the company. Business to business companies often don't need thousands or even hundreds of conversations annually with potential customers due to the high lifetime value of contracts, therefore low volume yet highly effective strategies can be an exceptional investment.

These strategies and ideas should be used for new and existing customers. Your know like and trust should be constantly building through exceptional delivery but you can bring in the above methods to increase the average spend of your customers, average number of times they buy from you and their overall lifetime value. Remember though, you cannot buy lifetime customers through marketing only, which is why understanding the level of conversations you can have in order to maintain quality levels is vital. If you use strategies to fill your boots with new business yet can't deliver, you will be on a seesaw and seesaws don't sell for high multiples of profit. The delivery quality and relationship you build long term with your customers, nudging them up the Ladder of Loyalty is where your profit really comes. Think back to our dog food business for a moment...

You may be thinking that this isn't marketing, but remember you want to build a valuable business with lots of lifetime customers. With that in mind, aren't your current customers, whom you have worked so hard to enter into a transaction with and who have already placed their trust in your hands, as important or even more important as generating new ones? Of course they are.

If this is the case and you know that retaining customers is many times easier than buying new ones, why do so many businesses fail to carry their relationships forward? It has been seen countless times that as soon as money and products are exchanged, the service drops. This happens continuously even with large brands, but some are fantastic at their further communication. Your current customers are a huge asset, so you want to understand how Raise Your Hand marketing works when managing those relationships.

At ActionCOACH, we teach the 6 steps to a better business as a way of gauging where your business is in regards to its journey to becoming a sophisticated enterprise that could work without its owner. The first step is Mastery, which is broken down into time, financial, team, destination and delivery mastery. The next step on the ladder is Niche, which is where your marketing plan lies. Your goal is controlled growth and consistent trust development. Conversational marketing will create control and allow you to choose the number of customers you can take on each month, day, week, or year without reducing your quality. If you do not complete mastery or are at least improving it consistently, then you will not see the magic that happens when you combine excellent product/service with amazing relationships. This is where your profit lies. The first step of Raise Your Hand marketing is generating more conversations than you have ever had before with new prospects. The second and far more profitable part is how you build and maintain those new relationships for as long as possible and do this through exceptional quality delivery and powerful relationship-building strategies.

Heading back to the bakery, they may receive a few DMs a week, and some footfall into the store based on their marketing strategies at present. They would likely not be conversing on anything other than a transactional level with their customers. With Raise Your Hand marketing, everyone is trained to be a conversation specialist, especially your sales people. The bakery's servers are sales people. They are the ones who are selling, at the end of the day. Teaching everyone how to communicate and gather data in order to either find need signals or create exceptional experiences based on the information provided is vital to Raise Your Hand marketing.

The switch to Raise Your Hand Marketing as an overall growth mindset will allow you and your team to improve communication and provide value to five or six times the number of people you are used to. Your DMs will be filling up and people will be in store redeeming offers. The new prospects you have are communicating with you and this is where the magic happens. By installing questions, simply focusing on providing solutions to needs, and providing excellent service, their prospects will want to be customers. This will allow for exclusivity and membership to be developed. If, however, the bakery tries to service everyone and becomes sloppy in delivery, one bad comment can undo huge amounts of work gone into the "know, like, and trust". If you have 50 boxes of eclairs and you have 60 people coming in, you will have 10 disappointed prospects who will loudly shout about it. If 10 people order a custom birthday cake from the 50 new lovers of your brand and they can only manage five at a time, five people are going to have delays and a crappy experience and their voices will be the loudest.

How many new customers can you handle each month?

Based on the conversation numbers you worked out in the initial chapters, this should allow you to have a basic view of the number of conversations you need, and if you want to grow, where delivery improvements are required to maintain a higher number of customers.

You need excess conversations in order to build massive want for your product or service. This want can be converted into membership and lifetime customers but servicing too many will move you backwards.

8

The Business Chassis

As the theory part of this book draws to a close, let's draw your attention to the business chassis or '5-ways'. This concept shows the general chassis that most businesses run from and allows you to express your numbers in a simple, easy to understand way.

Leads

x

Conversion Rate

=

Customers

x

#Of Transactions

x

Average Spend

=

Revenue

x

Margins

=

Profits

The business chassis, or '5 ways' as it is called in ActionCOACH, is five compoundable attributes that build a business. These are elements you can control which lead to the outcome you want. Leads are the first step of the chassis and many business owners do not feel like they are in control of their lead flow as much as the others. They feel like lead flow is actually an outcome rather than a controllable item. Raise Your Hand Marketing would agree with this, especially nowadays when competition is so rife and you are fighting for visibility on a much bigger scale. Raise Your Hand marketing brings control to lead flow, as it brings control to conversations and engagement. As long as you are conversing with the right people and you are maintaining a strong delivery quality, there will be a conversation rate and a conversion to lead. With what you are learning in this book, you can control conversations through time and money investments on a much larger scale, therefore creating easier tweak and edit possibilities. It's difficult to measure and make decisions on little data, and conversational marketing brings larger data to even the hardest of industries. By adding another layer to your 5 ways, you add even more control and an even simpler way to see the growth opportunities in your business.

Conversation (Completely
Controllable)

x

Leads

x

Conversion Rate

=

Customers

x

#Of Transactions

x

Average Spend

=

Revenue

x

Margins

=

Profits

You can control the level of conversations your business has. With what you have learned, the focus does not drop as you move them through the buying process of building trust and providing exceptional service; focus should intensify.

A definition of marketing is that 'marketing is every single piece of communication your business has with anyone'. This makes a lot of sense. You market for new customers, you market to your existing customers, and you market to your old customers but how your brand is portrayed to your creditors, banks, suppliers,and partners is also so important. They help make the boat go faster too and often, you can't do it without them.

Profitably buying lifetime customers with Raise Your Hand marketing comes in three stages and is linked highly with the Ladder of Loyalty. All of the common terms and theories you are tying during part one of this book are vital for your planning and execution. Patience is another skill that needs to be learned.

1. Initially Raise Their Hand (Buying New Customers)
2. Raising Hands For Customer Retention (Buying Repeat Customers)
3. Raising Hands For Lifetime Value & Referral Machines (Buying Lifetime Customers)

New customers, retention strategies, and referral strategies should form part of any marketing plan and education around marketing.

9

Common Mistakes

A recap of common mistakes - Chop some onions!

To close out part one, here are some critical areas we have discussed and mistakes often made when building out marketing plans. Through examples of past mistakes and standard issues seen all the time, you'll embed the theory and mindset better.

#1 Stop Trying To Get Married On The First Date

Remember Ben from the opening pages? Would you ask someone you find attractive, totally your type, the exact person you have been searching for, to marry you the very first time you met them? No? Occasionally, you have heard of this working, or seen a staged story line in a movie, but 99.99% of the time it doesn't. In marketing, why do you assume that this type of exchange will be successful?

How many times have you asked a prospect to engage with you the first or second time you interacted with them? I imagine it is a large number of times, if not most of the time when you initially interacted with your current customer base.

Have you been lucky so far? By focusing on the next date, not the marriage, Raise Your Hand builds a trusting relationship with prospects before the sale is made, allowing a more long-term relationship to form and ultimately a profitable lifetime relationship.

'Getting married on the first date' should now be quite clear. It's very likely that you are a little bit shocked at your behavior. That's in the past now, so move forward with the knowledge it doesn't need to be ever done again. What are the 'first dates' prospects have with your business? How many dates do you usually have planned before you ask for the sale? Are the buying signals that clear? If the buying signals are so clear, you are likely not having anywhere near enough conversations. That's an opportunity, not an issue, so get excited by it. Answering those questions will allow you to begin to visualize the prospect's journey.

In a business, offering prospects something they need and want right now is the perfect first date. The most important element of Raise Your Hand marketing, whether digital, virtual, or physical, is to open the door and have a conversation with them. By doing this you can have five or six times the engagement levels than before and with careful management, have people lining up at said door.

Note: As an example, a consultant we work with had a tough time getting anywhere with his pipeline, and sales were dwindling. He was exceptional at what he did, but did not know how to communicate properly, outside of the skill he provided, to build relationships with prospects and customers. His marketing consisted of a few referrals and a telemarketer who called to try and set appointments for him. The conversion rate was 1-2 telephone appointments out of 100.

Another example would be a bar, where the initial transaction is usually very easy to get if the prospect interacts with you. Marriage in this example would be in the form of asking someone to be a regular or bring their friends very early on. It may be a digital conversation in response to an offer. You can win the relationship by personalizing the experience from the moment they arrive for their offer or for their first experience. Maintaining your focus on the needs and wants of your customers will make marketing easier and lead to a cult-like following. In movies, you see that people have their own tables, their own experiences, and a relationship with the bar or restaurant. This is so powerful and very easy to implement.

The simple way to say this is as you will remember: give before you ask. You have to provide value before you ask for something. It's funny because that mindset is ingrained into us as children. You have to give before you can receive, yet in business you completely forget it…

#2 WIIFM (What's In It For Me)

One of the biggest mistakes made is not thinking about the customer, which should be obvious? Understanding WIIFM and using it for product/service wants as well as molding what your potential customers might want/need right now as a conversation starter is a key ingredient of this book. As you start to think about your first interactions with your target audience, your offering of this 'first date' is your first communication to suspects. These are people within your target market who do not yet know who you are/have not been communicated with before. It's your first chance to turn them into prospects, people in your target market who have shown interest in your first date offering. Your goal is to move as many of our target market into this prospect part of the ladder as possible, so your 'give' needs to be valuable and solve a problem they actually have, not something that suits you. This is where WIIFM is introduced, which is short for 'What's In It For Me', a marketing theory that is used to make us think about what our customers want at every stage of your interaction with them.

People are selfish and at the beginning of any customer journey. You are dealing with suspects who really don't owe you anything, who don't care about you, and who have no reason to buy from you. As you start to think about your very first interaction with your customer and how you are going to offer lots of value in return for a simple conversation opportunity, one you can develop, you need to aim for the heart and find something they want, need, and aspire to. Put yourself in your customers' shoes and ask yourself, "What am I getting out of this interaction?".

How much WIIFM are you including in your outreach? How much are you giving value before you ask for business?

When you start to incorporate these theories into your marketing plan, conversations, first dates, WIIFMs, you will see that these opportunities are everywhere, in your interactions with suspects and prospects, on social media, in how you interact with existing or potential customers. First, value, then ask. By following this methodology, you will be able to gain a huge advantage over your competitors and become loved by your target market.

#3 Selling the end goal WAY TOO SOON. Focus on the next stage of the process, not the end sale

As you begin to deploy strategies to increase conversations, it's important to keep in mind that at each stage your job is simply to move forward and gain agreement for the next date. Many people focus on the end goal, the sale of their product/ service, that they push prospects too far, too fast. It may take a little longer for the results to arrive, but they will be far greater than if you were to focus on the few that go through your sales process immediately.

Any exponential success requires patience. 'Small, seemingly insignificant improvements and innovations lead to staggering achievements over time' is the quote by Robin Sharma. Einstein said that compound interest is the 8th wonder of the world. That might be big thinking but it's the mindset that counts - the compound effect is everywhere.

When you think about the 'next stage', it's important to have these mapped out clearly before you go into the conversation step. You need to know what you are selling: the next stage. It's your job to get your prospect to raise their hand for the next conversation.

Learning from your mistakes

You have been introduced to conversations, what the true definition of a strategy is, mistakes you are likely making as well as the purpose of marketing as a fortress managing new, current and old relationships to maximize productivity. You have done a large number of reps, repeated key learnings and hopefully engrained some key mindset changes into your brain.

Please complete these questions before moving forward:

1. How many conversations did you have last week?
2. Where did these conversations come from?
3. What is your current 'conversation rate'?
4. Place your current pipeline and customer base into the Ladder of Loyalty?
5. What is your current acquisition cost?
6. What is the average lifetime value of your customer base across the last 12 months?
7. Are your current strategies more hunting or farming?
8. How much do you make on your customers' initial transaction and subsequent transactions?

Revisit the previous chapters and re-read sections to make sure you got it.

PART 2
PLANNING & STRATEGY

10

Your Goals - Starting With the End in Mind

Part two of this book will pull together the learnings from part one and help you put together the strategies to deliver conversations and drive your relationships forward.

As you begin to dive into planning and execution of Raise Your Hand strategies as a whole, it is important to position your plan in the correct way for your goals to become uncomfortable but achievable. A big goal is nothing without a clear-cut method of achieving it.

You may have heard the planning methodology that asks you to 'start with the end in mind'. This works by looking at your end goal and working backwards to now. This will enable you to judge how SMART your goals are. Marketing goals should and always should be process-driven, not outcome-driven. The end goals you set need to be created in a way so that the process can control the outcome. You learned that conversations are somewhat controllable, and the processes you set in place to create these conversations will be backed up by real data, allowing you to predictably judge how much work or investment will be required to achieve your goals. Process not outcome, conversations not sales. Processes are the tasks needed to achieve the goal you want; this is the final piece of the strategy formation you learned in the early chapters of this book. It goes target, offer copy, then the platform, then the processes needed to achieve it. This is either spend or time-orientated.

SMART stands for:

Specific - A specific goal should be tangible. You should be able to see it in front of you. It needs to be simple and sensible so you don't lose focus or motivation. A goal that you see regularly is something like 'I want to use LinkedIn to generate leads' or 'I want to increase my reach on social media'. Goals like this are not specific. Seeing our LinkedIn goal be improved as you work through SMART, the first improvement would be, 'I want to use LinkedIn to reach out to business owners to discuss how you might be able to help them'.

Measurable - Next comes the measurement element of the goal. The goal above of talking to business owners on LinkedIn brings some specifics into play, but it is still a long way from SMART. Adding measurability will make sure that you are edging a little closer. You would add this to the ''I want to use LinkedIn to reach out to business owners to discuss how you might be able to help them' goal by adapting it to something like the following: 'I want to use LinkedIn to send a message to every business owner in Denver'. This is measurable to an extent; it may, however, not be achievable.

Achievable - Sending a message to all business owners in Denver on LinkedIn? What for? How many business owners are there? How long will that take? It's important to be able to answer all of these questions. Remember, you now know what your basic conversation rate is and how many conversations you can have without creating detriment to the quality of your delivery. An improvement based on your data may be, 'I would like to message 1000 business owners in Denver'. This creates a significant goal and something that is achievable with real life data.

Results Orientated- Unlike non-marketing goals, where there may be more outcome-oriented statements, marketing goals, as you have discussed, should be process-oriented. To add results, our goal can be adapted to 'I would like to message 1000 business owners in Denver, in order to understand how many conversations you can generate from LinkedIn.' The result and outcome are now clear, and there is no pressure on this beyond delivering on the significant task. Adding time to this goal should finish it off and make it very clear.

Time Orientated - Adding time to your goals will create urgency and a destination. Destination master is often taught as the very first step in our 6 steps to a better business programme. Without a destination, it's difficult to maintain a consistent path. Our goal, without a time frame, could take years when it, in fact, should only take a few months. The outcome of achieving our goal used in the example is a conversion rate of conversations from LinkedIn. Over 1000 people, this will give us a good average conversion rate to create even smarter goals beyond.

Your smart goals should be big enough to make you uncomfortable but not too large that they will detrimentally affect your morale as well as your teams. If a goal is too big, it can compound in the wrong direction. For example, if your goal is segmented into daily tasks and a few days are missed, this can spiral into too much work and the goal will be dropped. This is made even worse when a goal is massively impacted by daily routine, which most are, as then the goal becomes unachievable. Remember, you always overestimate what you can achieve in one day, but underestimate what you can achieve in one year. Same goes for underestimating what you can achieve in one year and underestimate what you can achieve in ten years. The old phrase is 'eating the elephant, one bit at a time' and turning your vision into achievable, actionable things.

How does this relate to marketing and implementing Raise Your Hand strategies? Well, you need to know where you want to go, as this will act as the pin on the map your marketing machine drives towards. This goal will allow you to break down how many tasks you need to complete per week, typically the number of conversations, and then you can build the required strategies that will deliver said conversations. Beyond that, it's pretty simple to do, yet it will require discipline to achieve.

Your marketing plan should consist of SMART goals for each strategy you are looking to add to said plan. If you are an employment law firm in Toronto and are choosing an offer that will drive 10 conversations per week, then your goal would be backpedaled to the target, offer copy, the platform, and process linked together that you expect to drive this goal. 'Our goal is 10 conversations per week with business owners in Toronto. We will achieve this by asking for a conversation to use their expertise to form part of a new e-book on employment in Toronto. Our team will make 100 calls each week to raise 10 hands to achieve the goal.' That is a first date, you have your conversation, and you have content being developed post. Outlining the process needed to achieve your goal allows for daily activity to be monitored and measured, making tweaks every day, not every month, to increase the success rate of the hand raising strategy. Use the data you derived from your current marketing to do this, the conversation rate and the average number of conversations it takes to generate a new customer. You want these to improve, and they will, but as a baseline it means you are being conservative with your expectations.

Daily activity tracking is something the whole team can commit to.. This is usually a major BFO or 'blinding flash of the obvious' as it's called in ActionCOACH. A BFO is something you tend to look for in all education, something that stands out, an 'ah ha' moment. The BFO here is that if you include your in the planning process, have them set the goals and derive their time in a way they, in theory, decided, and then as an owner, you would receive a far more unconscious and conscious commitment to that plan than if it were me just planning it by yourself. The daily process allows for marginal gains to be made quickly and ensure that the strategies are easily manageable. Are you allowing your team to get involved with the planning and goal setting process for the business? If not, you should be. This is absolutely the same for decision making, decisions that directly affect the team and how the delivery of their role should be collective and include their opinions.

As an example, when I originally brought new ideas to Avalanche, it would often be 'my' idea and I thought that it needed to be implemented. I don't remember asking too hard or listening to opinions against it. By changing this and having our team involved, it becomes their project as much as mine. A business owner should never expect an employee to be as committed to a goal as them, but this will help. If you are a marketing manager reading this book, then involving the people who actually have to do the work will pay dividends long into the future, especially when it gets difficult.

Marketing is pretty much nothing without consistency. Consistency will be the lifeblood of any campaign and overall marketing plan, as you can't have clear measurement and therefore compounding without it. Consistency comes from commitment, discipline, and a plan, all three of which you cannot expect your team to deliver if they are not engaged.

When you develop a marketing plan, there will be a mix of proactive and reactive strategies. These strategies can pretty much be split up by using time and money. **Proactive strategies** are those that you can control. These are generally manual and time based, meaning you use your time to deliver them. Examples of these would be telemarketing, bold calling, leaflet drops, stands at exhibitions, etc. There is an element of cost attached, but you are still in control of how much activity happens and when. These types of strategies need the massive consistency discussed above, as without that they will fail. **Reactive strategies** are money based and generally are inbound enquiries received from prospects that have reacted to our advertising strategies, these are usually set up via investment into ad platforms, or other forms of media where reach is paid for. Your website and blog related strategy is also reactive as you have to develop the net and then the prospects will swim into it.

On the subject of fishing, proactive marketing is like heading out with your boat and rod/small net, seeking out those fish you really want and need. Reactive would be like anchoring large nets and allowing fish to swim into it. Reactive fishing costs more money because you are buying the time and equipment instead of using your own self or time.

Both proactive and reactive strategies can and should be focused on conversations. These conversations will enable you to create massive improvement opportunities all the way down your pipeline. They will also help you to make sure those big SMART goals you're about to set have a clear process. A marketing plan needs a mix of both proactive and reactive strategies and the theory remains the same. The success of each strategy will come down to the power of your offer and the immediate problems you are solving, which will in turn lead to reciprocation in the form of information and a relationship opportunity.

As your strategies are developed, goals derived, and processes mapped out, it's important you follow the SMART goal rules, whether the campaign is a proactive or reactive one. A huge mistake made by many marketing people is that deliverables are very weak in terms of their specificity and often are outcome deliverables rather than process-orientated. You, however, are beginning to think as a relationship manager and will develop a clear, process-driven plan with the outcome as your goal. Gone will be the boring reports about impressions or clicks, gone will be the trying to 'explain' your success to your superiors or your accountant as to why a marketing strategy is working but it isn't clear at all. The only deliverable our marketing plan will measure is hand raises & conversations. If a strategy does not have a clear hand raise deliverable, you will not include it. By doing this, you bring efficiency to your budget and have a clear communication trail to build on.

The common denominator throughout is that tracking and measuring success of strategies is long-winded, too detailed, and frankly, not worth the hours of time it takes for you to break this down. This will require a mindset shift, potentially in yourself as well as your boss if you're a manager. You can take this book to them and use it as your excuse to make reporting a LOT SIMPLER.

Your goals

So what is your end goal? To explain this phase, let's use an example business. This business is going to be called RYH Gardens Corp. RYH Gardens Corp is a landscaping company based in Las Vegas. The company has spent the last 20 years developing a strong team, yet has lived off of referrals for their work as well as some local advertising. The owners are looking to retire in 10-15 years, therefore want 'A big push' to grow their business. Currently, they do around $750,000 in annual sales and would like to get to $5M in 5 years to build an asset and enough profit to generate a good valuation ready for retirement. This is a big goal, but not unachievable, so they are going to break it down, working backwards from the $5M to now, putting processes in place to drive enough conversations based on their current conversation and conversion rates and average sale value.

The questions you need to answer to deliver this initial planning phase are the following:

- **Is your business a repeat revenue model at the moment?** *If not, then new conversations per month are vital, and you should think about introducing a recurring revenue stream into your organization.*

- **If you do have a recurring revenue model, how many times does someone purchase from you in 1 year?** *Average purchases are highly important. Measure this very clearly, and there should be various technologies available to your industry that will help with this question moving forward also.*

- **In order to generate 1 customer, how many sales proposals/sales pitches do you have to make?** *This is a SHOP-PER, as per our Ladder of Loyalty, someone who is talking about pricing and actually is a yes/no purchase conversation.*

- **In order to generate a sales proposal/pitch, how many conver-**

sations did you have to have? *This is the number of steps prior to them becoming a prospect. You haven't read into too much detail on conversations in their physical and digital form yet, but you should be able to deliver a rough idea here. As you launch your plan, this number will be very easily measurable. People tend to underestimate the number of conversations that they actually have, which you would define as two-way communication of some sort with a prospect.*

- **What is the average sale value per transaction?** *This should be the average across all sales. That, multiplied by the number of customers you have, is equal to the revenue generated.*

If you cannot answer the above right now, by simply answering these questions over the next month, you will have a huge ROI on this book and your time investment in reading it. There is a famous phrase, 'what you measure, grows' and it is very, very true.

In the case of RYH Gardens Corp the answers were the following:

- Their clients, on average, purchase 8 times per year. The company does not have a membership model but will look to include a subscription that will allow them to lock in further purchases.
- In order to generate a new customer, they have 3 quotes delivered on average
- In order to generate a quote, they have to have 4 conversations/2-way communications with prospects
- The average sale is $578.70, which equates to 1296 transactions across the year. With an average of 8 transactions per customer, this is 162 customers.

So RYH Gardens Corp's goal is to achieve $5M in turnover in the next 5 years. How many conversations do they need if they want to achieve a $5M turnover in the last year of their 5 year plan? Well, you first need to look at, based on today's average, how many customers they need. In the case of RYH Gardens Corp, they would need 1081 customers.

So in order to have $5M business, our 1081 customers would require 3243 quotes and 12,972 'conversations' with prospective customers based on their current numbers.

Let's head back to the 5-ways, a key system used by ActionCOACH all over the world that teaches business owners to focus on what they control. From a marketing standpoint, you can't just 'have' more customers, however, you can have more conversations and leads, just like you can have a better conversion rate by working on it directly. The 5 ways are below, so familiarize yourself with it again.

Conversation (Completely
Controllable)
X
Leads
X
Conversion Rate
=
Customers
X
#Of Transactions
X
Average Spend
=
Revenue
X
Margins
=
Profits

Now that RYH Gardens Corp knows how many conversations, in theory, it will take to generate $5M in sales from new repeat business customers, they can get to work and begin to come back towards now. A simple de-compounding can occur as you pull back to now and map your plan for the next year. If the goal is $5M, then your plan should be built on 5 Years = $5M, 3 Years = $2.5M, and 1 years = $1.25M. It is important to know that the compound effect gains momentum and speed as time progresses. It is also much easier to generate larger conversation numbers when there is stronger cash flow, as you have more experience, more network and, of course, more marketing budget.

Using the above model, RYH Gardens Corp is able to determine that in order to achieve a $1.25M business in the next year, they need to have 3,243 conversations. Now they can begin to set SMART marketing goals to deliver their required targets.

Remember! Do not over do it - Too many customers will reduce quality

It is a common mistake for many people to want massive success quickly. Get-rich-quick schemes have been around since money came into existence; you always want the largest success with the least amount of work. Farming and nurturing lifetime customers is not a get-rich-quick scheme, it takes dedication and expertise of your industry. Whilst conversations and great communication may bring a ton of single transactions, your service, ongoing care, and ability to scale will be the true test. One of the worst things to happen to organizations is growing too fast and then alienating customers, reducing their average number of purchases or how long they continue to be a customer. A reduction in RYH Gardens Corp with an average number of transactions by 2-3 times per year through slower delivery or worse communications would mean almost double the marketing and first time conversations that need to happen... It's compounding, and therefore, if it goes the other way it can hurt! Start with a target you know you can deliver on and then push the limits. Don't run before you can walk.

You should be happier to go slower, take reasonable steps and actually improve the quality of your service as you scale. That has to be one of your biggest SMART goals, improve service and customer retention as your business grows. If you can achieve this, there are boundless opportunities available to you. In any business you are involved in, quality has utmost priority alongside marketing, as well as innovation and standing out from your competitors. By simply offering a great service, communication, and after-sales care, you will often knock your competitors out of the park.

RYH Gardens Corp has a decision to make… Can they handle the level of customers needed to make their year one goal and retain the quality of their service throughout so it improves rather than declines? If so, then they can begin looking at offers to drive conversations. This is often the point where team and capital come into play. Some of you will have the luxury of being able to hire in advance of growth. You will all get to this point, but some of you will have to grow with cash flow. If that's the case, don't average it out cleanly across the 12 months of your plan. Start and build into it, increasing each month as you begin to grow and have the capital to support your operational needs.

RYH Gardens Corp is confident, so now they can begin to look at the strategies to drive those conversations…

11

Target, Offer, Copy - Finding Need

As you read earlier in the book, Raise Your Hand marketing is very simply, creating and managing a target market, offers, and copies that will create an 'I want that' feeling inside your prospects minds and a process that will allow you to reach the set group of people with time or money (proactive or reactive). This is the ONLY bit you can control during the initial hand raising process as you are not yet in a conversation with someone. Even during the conversation phase, where you are seeking need and solving problems via further offers and interactions (dates), building a relationship with your prospect and finding the need, either matching this to your product/service as a buying signal or supplying the need in return for a further conversation is the opportunity. There will always be a need that someone has, and if the prospects need does not yet manage or can be managed towards your product/service, more support for them is required in the form of know, like and trust in order to build value, so that when they are ready, they think of you.

When putting together a strategy, there is a simple formula put in place that will allow you to clearly define a plan for said strategy. By following this, you will be able to create a well-designed Raise Your Hand campaign out of any idea. Your Target, Offer & Copy is Raise Your Hand Marketing. The platforms you use will not change. This isn't some magic pill that will give you a special strategy that's going to pour cash into your organization. Marketing platforms very rarely change; only your target market can be tweaked, the offer and the way that you deliver your copy as well as the process you choose to distribute it.

Typically, Raise Your Hand marketing de-traditionalizes current marketing methods. For example, if telemarketing or cold calling is a well-used strategy in your industry, find out what the current average 'conversation rate' is. It is likely in the low single digits, as the standard and traditional way of telemarketing is to go for marriage, which is why it's an often hated platform by those who have to do it. By developing a Raise Your Hand offer and using ego and exposure opportunities across them, and portraying well in your process, you can expect to see this figure triple or quadruple relatively easily. This is because you bring it back a few levels towards an initial conversation and solving a wider market need, where you begin the education process for your target audience and build trust. You know already that ego & exposure needs are rife for nearly all B2B industries and emotion & aspiration for B2C. There may be others you can lean on, but you can be sure of increased success even if you only focus on those.

The first area to look at is your target. Defining your target market is relatively easy. This is actually more intense and past-data driven if you are B2B due to the fact that there are certain positions within organizations you need to target. People would argue that B2C is more complicated, with demographics, etc, but they are again overcomplicating for the sake of overcomplicating. If you are a marketing manager or manage a marketing manager, then making sure time is not wasted overcomplicating is vital.

12

Target Market Development

Take telemarketing as an example. You would like to use telemarketing to generate 10 hand raises per month that will lead to a conversation. In this strategy, the hand raise would be further action such as attendance to your store for an offer or perhaps a meeting that gives the customer something they need right now. Remember this from earlier chapters? Giving rather than getting? What do they need right now and how you can give that to them to enable a conversation to begin?

A great way to hone in on your target market and buying persona's are the following:

Problems

What problems do you solve? Are there problems that you may not have uncovered yet? It is likely that you aren't quite sure of all the problems you are able to provide a solution for, and creating this list is vital to your offer and copy development, as it allows you to truly define who your offer is going to be put in front of. When defining your target market using problems with Raise Your Hand

Marketing, you should look at wider market problems that you have expertise in.

A decorating firm whose key target market was commercial builders but did have a growing customer base of residential b2c projects they wanted to grow is a good example here. They knew that their b2c customer base was simply homeowners that wanted a professional paint job. The problem here is that most of their marketing was reactive, which cast a net to catch anyone searching for key terms around their area. This is good, but it isn't predictable, and they couldn't actively tell from a simple target market demographic who at this time needed a quote. Their proactive marketing approach was a guessing game which meant low levels of conversation and heavy effort. Two or three people out of one hundred would have the need and the efforts gone into putting their service in front of the hundred people meant the cost per conversation and eventual lead were very high. The problem solving element of target market definition and, eventually, the offer they presented needed to take care of the wider market instead, so they looked at the issues the wider market was probably facing. They came up with:

- **DIY** - A larger portion of the homeowner demographic would attempt DIY first, therefore they knew with their expertise they could provide free of charge support to DIY-ers at home.

- **Rectifying Mistakes** - A larger portion of their target market unfortunately had either DIY mistakes, mistakes from builders or mistakes from other decorators in their house. If content or support was provided to help rectify mistakes at low to no cost for the prospect, this would lead to high levels of reciprocation and word of mouth.

- **Budget** - It was derived from a short survey of prospects that did not buy that budget was an issue and a lower quality job, likely with mistakes that would eventually need to be rectified, often at a higher cost than the initial quote, was common.

If the decorator could tackle these problems with their new offers and weave in the two key b2c marketing tactics, which, as you know, are emotion and aspiration, they would generate far more hand raising opportunities. During the offer chapters, you will read about what they eventually put together.

Reverse Engineering Your Target Market

Reverse engineering your target market is a simple task that involves looking into who has purchased from you in the past. It sounds like an obvious thought process but is often overlooked. Who are your best customers? What positions are they in? How old are they? How did they originally engage with you?

Another reverse engineering technique is to look deeply into those who didn't purchase from you. Why was that? Many examples here will show you that you likely asked for marriage too early on when perhaps their need did not match your service. The problem, as you are now very aware, with marriage proposals is that you are guessing that the suspect is thinking and hoping that their need matches your service. If you take a deep dive into previous relationships and why they did not become customers, with honesty, you will find plenty of opportunities to improve your communication and steer away from those mistakes again.

Mistakes

Defining your target market shouldn't be that difficult a process as most of you have been in your businesses a while, but there is often a very narrow approach that you may be falling victim to. With most marketing focused on those who want marriage, now, the target markets are drastically reduced to a few percentage points in size compared to their original size. This is the reason marketing is not working.

Raise Your Hand marketing should give you a much wider audience to market to, especially if you are now thinking about the potential lifetime value of customers at different stages of their relationship with you. A small purchase now could lead to a significant purchase later on. The energy you invest into that smaller transaction and the care/love you give every person who interacts positively with your business will lead to big dividends later on. You never know who you are dealing with so having an abundant mindset will take you a long way in business. I am sure you have all heard of the horror stories of the beach bum walking into a car showroom and being turned away from a conversation, or the luxury outlet turning their nose up at the woman who doesn't fit their traditional buyer type only to highly regret it later on (queue pretty woman thoughts and guys, you know you thought of this too).

As you develop your plan and think about the size of your market, think 5% as your target initial hand raise number. So 5% of the people available to contact in your chosen market will raise their hand. You should be able to achieve a better result than this, but it will allow for a margin of safety and make sure that you have a large enough pool of suspects in this more defined target market to work with. If you want to achieve 1000 conversations this year, divide this by your margin of safety conversation rate, 5%, and you will have a number of 20,000. This means there needs to be at least 20,000 people in clear reach by your strategies in order for it to be feasible. If it is lower than what is available to you, you may need to rethink your target market. If your location doesn't allow for a different target market, then the value of your offer needs to be higher in order to achieve the level of conversations you require for your growth goals. The smaller the target market, the higher value your offer needs to be.

RYH Gardens Corp - Defining Target Market & Market Size

Coming back to RYH Gardens Corp, let's see how they developed their target market ready for offer development:

Following the margin of safety suggestion, and the knowledge that they will need

3243 conversations this year, which will lead to 811 quotes and eventually to the 270 customers. Multiplying this by the average sale of $578 and multiplying again by the 8 times average transactions in the year gives them their $1.25M target. You may be thinking that a large portion of their current customer base would be retained, which is correct should their service be excellent. There is also an opportunity to increase the effectiveness of their marketing by decreasing the number of conversations to get a quote and decreasing the number of quotes to generate a new customer. For the sake of simplicity, RHY Gardens corp will work their numbers out as new customers only. This will provide them with a large margin of safety and an opportunity to get ahead of their target early. As well as this, defining the problems and reverse engineering their target market, including those who didn't purchase, will provide them with issues and reasons they can develop offers to solve, likely leading to more trust, less objections and better numbers overall.

If you work your numbers out as the worst case scenario, you prepare yourself for the work at its toughest and therefore it will only be easier. If you overshoot and become too positive around them, your expectations will be off and you may get stuck behind the one thing you can't buy... time.

Multiplying the 3243 conversations by the 5% conservative suggestion provides RYH Gardens Corp with clarity that their target market needs to be 64,860 homeowners in the Las Vegas area. With simple research, it's easy to see that there are over 107,000 detached properties owned in the Las Vegas area. RYH Gardens Corp works to a roughly 35 mile radius, which adds an even better margin of safety.

RYH Gardens has defined its problems by reverse engineering as well as thinking about issues faced on a wide scale. If they were to market themselves directly using marriage proposals, the chances of them catching someone at the right time is low and the efforts required to get their conversations will be huge. They need to build a farm with wide-scale problem solving and carrying through exceptional service. They have other opportunities that will come out of this problem-defining exercise, which will be discussed later on.

Problem #1 - DIY - The DIY market in any of these types of industries is large. People are reluctant to spend, therefore there are often attempts to do work on their own. Instead of combatting this, supporting people who choose the DIY route would create a great, trusting image for the RYH Gardens Corp brand and when people do think, I need help, they will see RYH Gardens Corp as a trusted brand. Content & campaigns around the prevention of mistakes, tips, and free equipment for DIY users will be a great way to raise hands.

Problem #2 - Price Awareness - In a lot of industries regarding the home, people are educated wrongly about pricing points and how much things cost. With most of the target market not classed as wealthy, it's easy to assume that pricing will be a problem most people will face and pricing education as well as value will create a trusting image.

Problem #3 - Consistency - Most homeowners are aware their landscaping needs to be consistent, and the problem facing many is that they do it once, and then it gets out of hand. Consistency is deemed as expensive and the aspirational gardens out of reach. Solving this image problem will create lots of opportunities and it is also a great education tool to make people aware and put RYH Garden Corp at the front of people's minds.

Now you may be thinking, what about the people who just want a nice garden? Well, you are right but remember, your goal is to go wider market with your conversations. If RYH Garden Corp were to hunt for those only who wanted to spend the money right now, their marketing wouldn't be consistent, and it would be a lot of effort for little return. Solving the above problems will cater to these immediate needs and lead to high levels of conversation, which will create quick wins as well as set them up for long-term success. RYH Gardens Corp is not ignoring the immediate opportunities, just taking care and building trust with the market as a whole.

The offer development element of this book will be the largest. Some offers will not be relevant to you but still valuable reading. When you are making your plan, please come back to these chapters.

The offer that you choose will determine the success of your marketing strategy. The size of the need you are providing a solution for will determine the conversation rate. If you used telemarketing to give away a Ferrari in return for a conversation opportunity, their conversation rate would be 100%, not 1%, which is the current average for the professional services sector on a normal pitch based offer. This is obviously an obscene offer but it does provide a good visualization opportunity. The larger the want and the larger the solution, the higher the conversation rate. It really is as simple as that. The platform, as you can see, has not changed from telemarketing to something more fancy, only the offer. The platform doesn't change, you cannot physically affect the Facebook or LinkedIn platforms, for example. Your goal with offer development is to create varying levels of value, depending on budget, and try to make it as relevant to your future relationship as possible. If you do this in a way that uses the target market you developed in prior chapters and looks to solve wider market problems bringing in the key ego, exposure, aspiration or emotion marketing ingredients, you will have a much higher conversation rate.

This will be quite easy for some of you, especially if you are in a very transactional business like fashion or a low-cost service like hairdressing. For those of you who are in longer sales cycles or front of mind businesses such as law, where people do not need your service all of the time, then this is a little more difficult but very doable and more 'front of mind focused'. The below is split up into three areas, and you should be able to find yourself within one of these categories.

Transactional Offers (Needed products/services, short sales cycles)

Typically, a transactional business has a lower sale value but can be a very common purchase. This offer should be about winning trust and generating the relationship/love for your brand. This is a wonderful business to do Raise Your Hand marketing with; it's fast paced and fun. This offer is usually low cost to you, but creates a very grateful customer because the sales cycle is very short. Remember our discussion around the law 1of reciprocity? This comes thick and fast here, so you need to be geared up and ready for it.

An example offer here would be a hair salon. Once a relationship is formed between client and hairdresser, there is a fantastic opportunity for further purchases and a long-term relationship with that client. Therefore, what should the only goal be? Getting the relationship underway. Even if this costs money, you are buying a relationship opportunity. A typical offer, which can be used across various strategy types and platforms, would be giving away something everyone wants and 'needs' right now. This could be a free blow dry or free treatment, or something simple like a free 'damaged hair' consultation and repair to anyone that engages within our conversation from the chosen strategy. This 45 minute time investment could cost the salon $15-20, but the take up will be huge and stand out when compared to other salon marketing. If the copy is correct, this won't come across negatively and will create a bucket load of conversations and time with your team. In a large percentage of cases, if the service is to an exceptional standard, the hair salon will win the opportunity for a paid appointment and therefore the opportunity to generate a lifetime customer through service and ongoing customer marketing.

Another example could be a restaurant, where the lifetime value of a customer equally comes dramatically from your performance and your team's delivery. What drives restaurants faster than any advertisement could? Word of mouth. This, in a way, is Influencer marketing, something that many big name restaurants rely on. There is an example of a Vineyard and Winery where the owner created Instagram stations where beautiful photo opportunities were created; there were even signs saying 'Instagram station 1'. What happens when someone takes a photo and posts it online? They typically tag the restaurant. This creates know, like, and trust for you by leveraging the customers following, clout, and their experience. Offering to take photos of parties at tables, taking them with everyones phone and not just one as well as offering incentives for tagging the restaurant can all be powerful ways to turn all customers into influencers. What you should be looking for is performance opportunities, so you can wow your potential lifetime customers and run them up the ladder of loyalty. Restaurants are one of the best referral machines and gift giving businesses. They enable low cost trust building and movement of the customer. Your initial offer would simply be a first-time dining experience that is highly value added. The goal here is to get people in the restaurant and then wow them with the experience. You use aspiration and emotion by offering free value in return for things like image posting such as free drinks, food or tables. This allows access to a lifestyle that customers aspire to be like and works phenomenally and consistently. You build an offer that's low-cost but aspiring and drive traffic into your restaurant, using your service as a way to generate promotion, higher spend and trust with that new customer and their network.

A note on restaurants would be that there is a reason Michelin does their visits in secret (to an extent) as they would like to see a restaurant deliver their experience as normal. Exceptional service should be a standard, not a one off to impress a certain customer. This mindset should be built into your whole delivery programme, and in theory, any business should be acting as if their version of the Michelin man is arriving each day. Even if you are not in the restaurant business, you can learn from the perfection and process-driven behavior of Michelin star chefs. I would recommend reading and watching some of the documentaries available on the likes of Youtube which follow these restaurants as they seek these fabled stars. It's a deep insight into how the best treat their product, their customers and the overall experience.

Typically this is found in business-to-business companies where the sales process is a drawn out set of meetings, calls, or proposals until both parties align on the engineered outcome and price. Typically, Raise Your Hand Marketing is very effective at driving higher than average performance from notoriously low yielding platforms and strategies.

The offer for a business-to-business company again has to be centered around something your potential customers need and want right now. You can engineer an offer that will provide that to them in return for a conversation. By now, you should have a clear idea of your cost per acquisition and based on your conversion rate, some idea of how many conversations you will need to generate a sale, therefore your targeted cost per conversion. With the sales cycle driven offer, you will typically use a time-based process like 'number of calls' or 'number of emails' keeping process costs low, therefore you should have some budget available to create an offer/lead magnet that is going to make an impact and get hands being raised.

The phrase 'lead magnet' is a common one, it is often attached to physical documents or gifts, but in reality, a lead magnet is anything that drives a lead towards us. Building the correct lead magnet for your industry is an art and does take testing and measuring. You need to get into your prospects head and create something of value that will make an impact and connect said prospect to you further. Creating a few is smart, and this will be one of the driving differences in your campaign's success. The strategy to reach people is only one element; how you draw them towards you is key. You may not get this right the first time; however, this could be the determining factor as to whether your 'strategy' works to the best it can. The next chapter will show you various forms of lead magnet and give you some ideas. Remember, the higher the perceived value, the higher the conversation rate and law of reciprocity.

You have to remember that business success is about process not outcome. This is where the management of marketing agencies goes wrong, the management of marketing staff goes wrong and, the management of your overall business goals goes wrong. Process is controllable, the outcome is not. If you focus on the outcome over process, you will inevitably not perform to the best standard. Defining the correct offer, out of all of the processes (target, offer, copy & overall strategy), is the most vital.

When developing a lead magnet in a multiple meeting/proposal based company, are pitching and meeting multiple times for a single purchase.

This exercise below is a great way to determine how to build the correct lead magnet. You will be familiar by now with the terms and should have your numbers freely available:

1. Average Acquisition Cost

Our acquisition cost to date should play a factor. What is it? If you have this figure, how much would you be happy to pay for a conversation? You know now how many conversations on average in the last year it took to buy a new customer, so defining an initial budget for your lead magnet will be simple. Determining what you would be happy to purchase a customer for is a major step in building your lead magnet. Remember, in this section you are talking about a longer sales cycle, so time and opportunity cost become a factor. If done correctly, then because of this, you can create a VERY low conversation cost, which will then allow you to invest more time and energy into the close. If the lead magnet does its job of beginning to build trust, then you will be well on your way to success. You now know that the first transaction is the hardest, the 2nd is the most valuable, and customers who purchase twice are far more likely to purchase again. The management of your prospect during their first transaction will be a determining factor of whether they buy again. It's more at this stage a matter of quality and service, therefore your financial firepower should be focused on the first transaction.

Let's say that your acquisition budget is $400 per new customer. This is the cost of your marketing and time to generate a customer. Obviously, the lower the better, but when you know your figure and include the knowledge of lifetime value, you can paint a picture on what you want to spend to buy a new customer. However, for growth and due to the mindset change around lifetime value, it may be that you want to increase your budget vs your current acquisition cost. Decide on this budget with these things in mind.

A lot of people will simply divide the marketing costs (Yes, including the sales and marketing people and yes, this should include your time also to the best of your ability) by the number of transactions, this creates a cost per transaction. Whilst this is correct, it will bring your figure down from its true acquisition cost. Your true acquisition cost for the sake of buying lifetime customers is the marketing and sales costs divided by the number of new customers per annum, less any costs you can factor in for repeat business. Due to the type of business being discussed here, the 2nd transaction should be very low or no cost and based on your relationship. If you are transactional though, your secondary purchase strategies will have their own acquisition cost.

Determine this figure to the best of your ability. As you progress, you can develop tighter acquisition cost management and do this per strategy. Well done if you are already doing so.

2. What problem are you solving?

This was touched on during the last chapter on targeting. Find a problem that your prospect needs to solve now. For example, if you are a software developer, offering a free problem solving service would be a sort of lead magnet, or UX/UI critique for example. Problems are faced in your industry all of the time, some of them wider than others and some not directly linked to a service/product you offer but relevant to your expertise. This is the time to put yourself in your clients' shoes. You know your acquisition budget, so develop something of value your customers need right now, even if this means investing into that value. In the coaching business, coaches often give away books or courses to solve specific problems. This carries a cost, but it provides their client with something they often are very thankful for, creating the first stage of the law of reciprocation. This isn't that exciting, and it's low on the perceived value scale but it will provide a better engagement than simply asking for marriage. You only want an introductory conversation at this stage, so it's not a huge ask. The higher the value of your initial offer though, the more conversations you will have. You have all seen companies go absolutely nuts with this in the past. There is a reason why boxes at stadiums, hospitality areas and 'entertainment' roles exist. These are, in theory, relationship builders and high perceived value that have nothing to do with the business at hand but is something that their customers want, badly, leading to a very high rate of hands being raised and extended relationship building opportunities.

I once was invited to the final of a soccer game at Wembley by a company I had interacted with for a very small amount. I had a great time and spent 2 years in a relationship with that business. This may be big for what you are discussing right now and for our marketing strategies but this type of business is very relationship based.

For example, if you are a car sales business. Your optimal client may be individuals with multiple cars and reasonable net worths, and perhaps there is a race or event nearby that would be worth bringing the top 10 potential customers based on demographic? Offer it as a networking opportunity (This is valuable to people in that net worth). Would this end in an opportunity for you to converse with them all? Would individuals raise their hand to his? Likely.

Another example would be if you were a coach. Who are the most famous speakers coming to your town? They cost $300 to see speak, why not invite the 10 optimal clients to go and watch all expenses paid? Ballsy, but it would work. Would you end up having great conversations? Absolutely.

3. Physical or digital?

The above examples are on the higher end of our approach and a lot of businesses feel like they wouldn't have the capital for, and that's ok, you are building your business after all. You should hold these big ticket items in your arsenal for the future. They are an easier way to ensure your strategies work for you and get hands raised at a higher rate than marriage. Generally, if the lead magnet is that good, you will have a queue of people creating even further conversation opportunities for you outside those who actually get the opportunity. Starting out, there are ways to create lower-cost lead magnets for each strategy to see what it does to the conversation rate. Even the low-cost examples of e-books, events, or whitepapers providing information that is more wide market focus does far better than your accustomed sales approach. Generally digital lead magnets are used with social media as a way to create some automated interaction and create either form fills or DM conversations. Guides, tip sheets, and practical tools to help customers solve a problem have all worked very well for this type of business. Lawyers, accountants, software, etc, are good examples where information and problem solving examples are valuable. You will struggle to find an industry that a well put together tool of value couldn't be put together at a low cost. Physical lead magnets cost more money but they very rarely do not end in a valuable conversation, so it's going to be a matter of budget that helps you make that decision.

Front of Mind Offers (Not an every day requirement)

Front-of-mind marketing is a tricky and challenging environment. This falls into the category of businesses where their services or products are requirements, but not all of the time. This is a practice of patience and consistency. A real estate agent, for example, may deal with their customers once every seven years. The number of real estate agents whose communication is, therefore, once every seven years or when the customer needs them is incredible. This used to be all too common, businesses are better these days at taking care of this but they are in no way doing enough or doing it in the right way. Front of mind is best split into two categories:

1. Very long repeat purchases

What do the greatest businesses in industries with very long sales cycles such as real estate or car dealerships have in common? They deal in emotion. Emotion may be the single most powerful tool in a marketer's arsenal, especially if you are a consumer brand. Emotional engagement with your customer will allow you to beat your competition time and time again. Your emotional attachment is their goal, the purchase is special and the time in between purchases is special. You make them feel a part of you. The same tools used here should give you inspiration no matter what type of business you run and it's an exciting/thought provoking section of this book.

I bought 2 Porsche's from 2 separate dealerships. One dealership ended up receiving 5 referrals from me as well as multiple other purchases from my family, plus I will be working with them again in the future. Now Porsche did a lot of hard work in the 70s, 80s, & 90s with their current target market, yes, they thought that far ahead, instilling the aspiration to drive a 911 later on in life, they didn't need to 'sell' me per se, but I believe Porsche know that and they know that this marketing has created an opportunity for a lot of 1st-time customers but will they come back?. Now as a younger Porsche driver and in the extremely lucky position to buy such a car in my early 20s, I was very much looking forward to going through the buying experience. These were, after all, sub-dealers of the main brand. My purchasing process was smooth, conversation driven and I spent a lot of time discussing with the sales representatives, it was what you would expect from such a purchase. My delivery, just like the other car you bought was great again, just like you would expect. The difference came between how these dealerships continued their relationship. One called me to ask me how I was doing about 1 year after my purchase. Since buying, I had no communications and the call went along the lines of 'you are seeing if you may want to discuss another car as the supply chains are very long at the moment', the conversation didn't last long. The second dealer invited me to a track day event at Silverstone. On the track day, I spent time with drivers, Porsche owners and joined the Porsche club to meet and network with other owners. I spoke for hours with various teams, enjoyed the cars and felt special the entire time. I left a complete raving fan. This happened on multiple occasions and probably cost them three or four hundred dollars to do but the power of enjoyment focused on the reason why I bought in the first place was phenomenal. One of the sales team knew I was in business and invited us to use their conference rooms overlooking the Porsche showroom for a few of our events, creating even further relationship opportunities. The final straw and likely the most british thing you will read all day is that when passing by I popped in to chat about a new car, the team invited me and my partner (As well as her parents) to sit in the showroom and watch the royal wedding with them, as well as watch the delivery of the GT2 RS that was arriving into the garage, stickers and all. These things do not cost money, they cost care only. They didn't need too, they have many customers a hell of a lot richer than I am, but this installment of care for even the smallest of customers showed me how it's done.

Your long sales cycle and opportunities to care for your customers and celebrate why they are buying from you in the first place is your opportunity to create a great offer. You cannot compete on price, so compete on their story, not yours.

So if you are in a long sales cycle business and you are looking for new prospects, focus on retaining emotional attachment, bring further aspiration into play, focus on why they would come to you. Do not just say 'great' service, show your current customers and create opportunities for emotional experiences for your customers. If you are a mortgage broker who is struggling to generate conversations in a price competitive environment and want first time buyers of homes, perhaps it would be beneficial to host a first time home buyers event, and invite people to have their questions and worries answered, creating relationships. You cannot price compete in this type of business, and often people will buy from the same businesses over and over due to their relationship. Finance is a typical ego based business also. People feel like they have 'their financier', which is all the more opportunity for you to make them feel special. Make sure that when developing the strategies in the next chapter that you clearly think about this.. If you won the first purchase on price, then make sure you are building emotion, aspiration, ego or exposure opportunities for the customer constantly depending on your industry.

2. Needed, but not all of the time and maybe only in emergencies

A company that falls into this category of front-of-mind marketing would be a lawyer, insurance specialist, or someone who deals with things like pest control or some sort of care in the event of an issue arising. They are almost always 'necessary' businesses, which puts them in a great place to be successful, but these 'necessary' businesses again often end up being treated like commodities and there is always someone or some technology looking to undercut you. Truth is, people are lazy and most of your competitors would like to think they aren't but they are. You can quite easily out communicate and out 'value' your competitors with just some simple consistency. The trick with this type of offer is very simply to generate data hand raises. Get their information and permission to receive value from you. This will allow you to be front-of-mind, so that when they are ready, you will be the person they turn to. If you can build in some emotion and develop a relationship along the way, then you can build almost certainty into generating the business when it arrives. For the first interaction though, which the bulk of your plan will be built on at this stage, you need volume of value. If you are a lawyer, you would use the Raise Your Hand theory of giving away what your prospects need now. What questions does every prospect have you can answer? What is something that your prospect always needs that you can use your experience to develop cost-effectively? The answers should be pretty simple to create. Your offer is then very simply to give this value away, as much as possible and then build on it over time. What this does is make sure you are there in their mind so when the need arises or they think of the problem, your business is the one to turn to. Here is an exercise, think of a problem you may face, it could be any problem or a question you may have? Does a business or person come to mind that would be that solution to your problem? They likely do. Now think about whether that business is actually consciously trying to be front of mind for you? Most of the time the answer to that question is, 'they may be but I doubt they are really thinking about it'.

Now imagine if you really thought about it for your business?

'Know, Like & Trust' with offers

There will be a large number of stages to your customer's journey with you. The need for layers of trust to be built, through the customer's experience with you, will allow you to lean on bolder more valuable offers as time passes. The initial offer can be all you need if you are a fast transaction business, food being an example. Everyone needs to eat, therefore you are competing for something everyone needs and are pretty much thinking about all of the time. Food is still a perfect business to bring emotional and aspirational firepower into play, though. In this business, it's about expanding the target market rather than initially building relationships. The goal should be to get the prospect into the location, then build the trust through the businesses personality and service.

Have you heard of conscious and unconscious competence? This is a good lesson for business owners, marketers and professionals in general. Being unconsciously competent, in general, means you know how to do something without thinking about it. The polar opposite is unconscious incompetence, meaning you are unaware you don't know how to do something. It is recommended that you read up on this subject in a little more detail to understand the psychology behind it. With marketing and trust, you are seeking unconscious trust. The act of trusting you without thinking about it. As a prospect, the person has conscious distrust of your business. You haven't earned their trust yet. As you develop your relationship with them, this will move into a conscious state of trust. Then, as further relationships develop, this will become unconscious and asking for referrals or testimonials is something they wouldn't even think about, as well as trying new products/services, spending more money and becoming more of a valuable customer. This type of trust takes good service and massive value. By starting this early and in a big way, you can ensure that the person's trust journey is already well on the way by the time they even purchase.

What's the common denominator with offers?

The common denominator with any Raise Your Hand offer is using your target audience to determine a need that said target audience will raise their hand for.

The self-identification process of this, be it a very simple social media post about engaging with a poll or a full blown ad offering a call to action around a free voucher, will create the law of reciprocity and lead to a two way communication. If it doesn't, you need to re-think your offer and what you are asking for in return. These can be big, these can be small, they can be cheap, they can be expensive. How well you determine your customers' needs will be the determining factor between a strategy you launch, i.e a social media ad strategy, being disappointing or not. A monkey could run your ads for you if the offer was good enough and it provided enough need. For the likes of telemarketing, where the traditional calls completed to lead generated is 1-2%, this is completely down to the need I am providing a solution for. Not a chance is that 1-2% strategy offering any give or providing any solutions in an abundant manner. If I was to give away a ferrari for

13

The Different Types of Offers

In this chapter, you will be guided through specific offers & examples that will act as thought provokers when developing your offer. These make up the most vital element of your marketing plan and really where your ideas come alive. The offers described in this chapter are still different from the platform, which will come next, but you will leave this chapter with a knowledge of what's available and how Raise Your Hand marketing can work in your business. This cannot contain all types of offer, so head to our website in order to submit something our strategists can review if you cannot find what you are looking for.

As you are reading this, think clearly about how you could adapt the idea for your business and whether or not it would be the right thing for your industry.

Not all offers will be included here, but enough to get your mind flowing. The key is figuring out what the prospect needs and finding a way to put it in front of them. Use these offers as guidelines and if there are other distribution methods you have in mind, just bring in the theory and see how it fits.

A few words on content:

The first thing to think about here is the difference between permanent and temporary content. This includes social media posts, blogs, videos, website pages, etc. What's important at this stage is to make sure the bulk of the content is permanent, which means it's leveraged. If you're familiar with ActionCOACH you will know that leverage is an extremely important part of any business. The definition of this is 'ever more with ever less'. This can often be phrased as do the work once, receive the benefits indefinitely or permanently in this case. Permanent content will remain at the forefront of whatever platform you post it on indefinitely and will not get lost within the hyperactive nature of most content platforms today.

What is the lifetime of a tweet? What is the lifetime of a Facebook post? What is the lifetime of an Instagram post?

Tweet - Half life (Time it takes for the tweet to have 50% of its power) - 20 minutes
Facebook Post - 24 Hours
Instagram Post - 48 Hours

On the flipside, what is the lifetime of a YouTube video? What is the lifetime of a blog post? Or a website page?

Youtube - Minimum 20 days, compounds over time with engagement and can build viewership for years.
Blog - Upwards of 2 years
Website Pages - Indefinite subject to the quality of the content in line with Google's SEO rules

Using social media platforms is obviously very important, but a lot of them, oddly where you see people spending most of their time, are the shortest. Permanent, valuable content will allow you to create a permanent foundation for your future marketing. If, for example, in 2 years time, you looked at youtube and your business had 100 videos that showed various valuable opportunities, stories, client referrals, and more over that time, would that be an amazing opportunity for you to showcase further? As permanent content remains and is marketed, it compounds and will help you in building that ever important trust later on. Trust, as you know, is a key factor to your long-term success and the faster you build trust, the faster you make the sale.

When developing what content you will be using in your marketing, it is suggested the bulk of the focus be on permanent content i.e. your videos and blog. Then, your temporary content i.e. social media posts should be link backs to permanent content which will include further hand raise opportunities for prospects. Instead of making your posts singular online, try to create multiple engagement opportunities.

This is called content curation. It's the act of creating major foundational content that is permanent and then creating shorter snippets from this for your more fast, impactful content on social media.

Raise Your Hand marketing is leveraged. Your campaigns and strategies should create multiple assets. A huge portion of the conversational strategies create content as a bi-product. Good content shouldn't need to use half the time in your marketing budget, so think about how you can take care of these things at the same time.

Ebooks

Ebooks are a long-form piece of content that can act as a great Raise Your Hand as they dive deeply into various problems your prospects face on a regular basis. As with any offer, the plan will be to ASK our prospects if they want it and get them to identify as interested. By focusing on a problem you know is wide-ranging, you can be sure to hit big with your conversion rate of people raising their hands and saying 'YES, I would like to receive your Ebook'. The great thing about E-books is their ability to sit behind forms, so you will be able to form part of both our proactive and reactive strategy plan when you choose our platforms. You can either ask manually or put the advertising budget behind it and guide people to the download opportunity.

A copy for an e-book ad could be: 'Are you an executive in Montreal? It was found that nearly all executives don't know their rights and therefore would obviously benefit from a simple, legally backed tip sheet. Would you like a free copy? Just send us a DM with 'executive' and you will get one right to you.'

Another route for more detailed and experience based industries are whitepapers. A whitepaper is defined as a long-form piece of content, that is more research based and detailed. Not all marketing has to be tips or short-form burst content. You could write a longer piece to aim more at the veterans of the industries you are trying to target or the more detail oriented prospect. One thing that is fantastic about whitepapers is they're a great way to showcase expertise, ideas and your past client stories in a non-salesy way. The same trick of asking gets you a good uptake. Another idea that enables us to add the 'double' or 'triple' asset to this offer (remember, you want to make sure our Raise Your Hand work is delivering at least two or three benefits at once) is collaborative content. Remember ego? Well, a collaborative whitepaper with a potential strategic alliance (or potential customer) will allow for a stronger, more varied whitepaper as well as the golden brand collaboration opportunity. Both brands on the document and almost certainly some reach from the collaborator sharing the work when complete. You could include experts from other fields and will do interview style calls with them in order to get their feedback on topics. This interview would give you a golden conversation opportunity with someone meaningful, but it can also be turned into video content if structured well. Then when complete, your brand is permanently connected to theirs and will get a higher hand raise uptake than just content written by yourself. What have you achieved? A strong expertise driven document you can promote, various relationship conversations, video content potential, brand collaborations and increased reach. Isn't that interesting? The same goes for other downloadable content like guides or tip sheets. Collaborate as much as you can and generate many low-cost assets for your business.

Articles/Blog

Marcus Sheridan often talks about having a 'learning center' or something of the sort on your website. This permanent content allows for know, like, and trust to be built quickly and gives you the opportunity to answer questions before they're asked. Every question answered, with brutal transparency, even if it is answering criticism creates trust. When it comes to using blogs for marketing proactively, instead of it being a big net, you can drive blog traffic using Raise Your Hand marketing. This is done in the same way as all content. It is written in a way that solves a wide market need or answers a question that people have. This then when distributed on ad platforms, organically or via the search engines with key words will increase the click flow to your blog and website. But what is an article? It is typically a longer format content piece that focuses on a part of your service offering or expertise. The issue you see with a lot of types of this content is that businesses tend to focus on them instead of their potential customer and the challenges they are facing. Do you sell home lease renewals, for example? Instead of writing about a lease renewal, which can be pretty boring, instead you could write a blog that states '5 mistakes that cost the average renter thousands of dollars' or '5 easy tips to protect yourself against your landlord'. You know all of this stuff and it focuses on a problem and solution. As a proactive Raise Your Hand offer, this article would be advertised as a private article which could be sent upon the prospect raising their hand. Alternatively, you could include a larger offer in the article such as a 'free lease review'. Moving people from your first date to the second date and a conversation needs to be your goal so make sure the blog is written in the way this is an easy next step.

Building your call to action or 'conversation' is again just about determining value and using your budget to apportion funds to the offer value. Depending on how much lifetime value you want to provide, in the case of the attorney above, they could even go as far as suggesting giving someone free attorney for their next lease review. Typically these happen once every year, and renters move more often, so you know that buying a customer with say a $250 time cost will lock in a great relationship. Once the relationship is done and they are thankful, they are prime for further marketing and you will be front of mind for the next time they are in need of help. I wonder what else they could need? A will perhaps needs doing, or maybe there is a referral opportunity. Raise Your Hand marketing is all about how you raise hands and continue raising them until you have raving fans. The more you invest at the beginning, creates more critical mass and relationships which in turn creates stronger long term relationships. Patience, however, is key.

How could you leverage problem solving articles to your benefit?

Competitions:

One of the best Raise Your Hand offers has to be competitions. They can be highly successful in generating thousands of new contacts and millions of dollars of revenue as a direct result. Competitions work well for businesses with consumer products but they can work nearly just as well with business to business customers. This can happen in two ways:

1. Your own product

If you have a product that is very popular, yet you need to break through the noise, or potentially your target market is difficult to define due to it being a very wide margin, then you can create a high ticket competition to drive both following and lead flow. With any competition, make sure it is something that people actually want and could use right now, and don't scrimp on the value. The higher the value the bigger the success.

If you are B2C, this should be very easy for you to develop. An example would be the Bakery from part one of this book. They could create a competition that would be 'free sausage rolls for a month' or something like a 'birthday cake'. These have relatively low development costs but always succeed in getting hands raised. The call to action would simply be engagement on social profiles or form completions. If the competition's value is high, go for the form completion.

In the case of RYH Gardens Corp, they could develop a competition that is very high ticket such as 'win a garden makeover worth $5000'. This would drag some serious attention to it, with the form being used to gather data such as size of garden, current landscaping, and whether they have help at current as well as aspirations. The key to generating more data is to generate more reciprocity and the higher the value, the higher the reciprocity.

2. Other people's products

Any business, even if your product/service isn't exciting enough to give away in a competition, can use this offer to drive higher following online and create great strategic alliance opportunities. The best way to explain this is by a real example.

I used to be a shareholder in a kitchen brand you were looking to rejuvenate after a string of bad managers and owners. There was little money available so I wanted to put this to work in the best way possible. I reached out to a famous influencer who I knew was just about to begin a major renovation. She offered, in return for a major discount to post about the product and help us build a wide reach, quickly, something you desperately needed. This was going to cost us a lot of money but I quickly removed the anxiety by focusing on one thing, trust. This person had 1.3M loyal followers, a large number of which fit our industry. It was worth the investment. Most companies when doing influencer marketing get so caught up in the posts and big reach they forget to collect data and get hands raising/interacting with your brand more than just checking out your page. The latter is great but you *can make it a lot stronger. I reached out to one of our suppliers, a very famous kitchenware brand who you had done some work with in the past. I asked them if they would be open to giving, yes giving, us a prize for the launch of our influencer post. They agreed, giving us a $600 stand mixer to give away as a prize. All the prospect had to do was to follow both parties and due to the size of the prize, fill out a quick form. Ofcourse, the form had a series of questions to help us analyze them and mark those in target and those not. As well as this, you put a free consultation checkbox as a required yes or no for each entry. The influencer loved the idea and you were a go. After one day, you had over 1200 applications for the competition, and each party had gained the equivalent in new followers to their instagram page. Of the 1200 applicants, 138 of them clicked the free consultation box which when followed up with turned into 81 scheduled meetings. The 81 meetings were in fact more qualified meetings than the company had had in the 18 months prior and coupling that with the prospects received via people downloading our bro-chure due to the posts, you ended the week with over 200 shoppers. Would I have paid for the stand mixer? Absolutely. What happened to our relationship with the supplier? We worked together a lot and they even used our showroom as a photoshoot location and I am often in contact with the marketing director 3-4 years on, despite having sold my interest a year or so later. The ability to cap-ture 1200 prospects, perfect for further marketing and over 200 people deemed as shoppers transformed the business and the influencer articles and posts made them very easy to do business with. All in all, the marketing campaign cost me about $35,000. It generated well over $500,000 worth of business in its first year.*

Influencer marketing is an overall strategy in itself, but as discussed a few times, strategic collaborations are a form of influencer marketing, just on a smaller scale than a celebrity. You are still utilizing someone's love and trust for another brand to enhance your own. For a solid competition with enough entries to make you excited, aim for a $500 price tag retail so it's chunky enough to get people aspir-ing to win. This does NOT need to be anything to do with what you sell, it does however just need to be a product with the same target market as you. A lawyer for example could giveaway a retreat stay at a luxury hotel and the copy could be centered around 'beat the burnout' or they could link up with a local race car track and the copy could be, 'Thinking time reduces simple mistakes that often cost thousands to fix (trust us, you know), so you have linked up with X track to give one an executive a day out learning how to drive a race car'. The opportunity is that your relationship with said supplier grows and you are instantly associated with them, the branding is also permanent and you can leverage it further by creating permanent content around the experience. Price tags like these will cut straight through the target market noise so make sure to really think. If it's great, your ad take up will be huge for little money and if you are doing manual outreach, this will be very very easy.

Video offer

With video, you need to understand the difference between explainer and educator. You need explainer content on your site that goes through what you do and the results, accompanied by the written version. You need as many FAQs as you can think of, both video and written. This type of content is key 'They ask, You Answer' territory, which is a book we recommend by Marcus Sheridan, who just so happened to be the co-speaker at the UK book launch of 'Raise Your Hand Marketing' and a great theoretical alignment for this topic.

For Raise Your Hand offers, think about video as an educational tool for potential prospects. This takes some thinking but nearly every industry can develop videos like this. The key, again, with any Raise Your Hand offer is to ask someone whether they would like it. This gives you a conversational opportunity from the outset. If only a small number of people take up your offer, the likelihood is that it is not powerful enough. Video education is great for those industries where content is stale and your competition particularly shys away from education. Typically, this is due to them not wanting to give away the 'secret sauce' and this closed mindset will be an amazing opportunity for you to capitalize on. Let's say you are a hair salon and you want to engage with customers more/create a series that will educate them. You know this will lead to better treatment of hair and also bring you and the customer closer. If you filmed a video series on how to care for coloured hair and asked customers or new prospects via an ad if they would like to see it, would you get a response? Potentially. People also love being asked for help, so a way to enhance this series would be to say something like, 'We need your help! If you have coloured hair, you would love for you to watch our 5 video series on caring for coloured hair and give us your thoughts.' Let your hair do the talking. For those that give us an honest review, you will in return give you a free blowdry and treatment experience worth $50. Just DM us to help!'. This makes sure people get involved and will also give you golden relationship opportunities with prospects and customers.

I owned a hair salon once and you doubled the number of transactions in less than 3 months using a very similar system. Seeing as you have discussed law a bit in the last few chapters, this industry could focus on walk through videos of key stages of the year. One could be a walk through video of how to read an employment contract and what to look out for or it could be a divorce walk through with everything they need to consider. Focus on educating needs and you will get hands raised, consistently. Video is also a fantastic permanent content addition to your marketing plan. Again, lot's of opportunity for double and triple asset strategies here.

My 30 Day Wealth Challenge is a great example of a Raise Your Hand offer. I have built a great course with stacks of value on a subject people often have problems with. Typically when you ask people if they would like this coupled with various sign up offers, you get engagement due to its high value.

Events

Now the topic of events is currently a lot more relevant in the B2B industries, especially those in the education/coaching industries. This is because there is so much education available at the click of a button that it's harder to break through the noise. If your event is niche, this can be stronger. An event is typically set up as a talk/launch of some sort and can be highly effective for your business. Testing whether or not your event is set up correctly, positioned correctly or gives enough value is pretty easy though. Simply asking people, ideally outside of your current raving fan network (They will always come, which is great, but you want to buy new customers as well) should give you a clear answer. The suggestion with any RYH offer is big value, investment from you and problem solving, preferably more than one. If you can put these together then you will do a lot better.

An example would be for an accountant who wants to host an educational seminar. Most people can look this up online so you need to position it slightly differently with the same outcome. This would usually be the accountant being able to speak about something and get hands raised in the room, another offer that needs to be thought about. Firstly, focus on local networking or luxury networking depending on the focus bringing in multiple reasons why people would want to attend. Yes, cater for the education, as long as its niche and the problem is very clear with your event providing a solution. In our accountants case, this could be about tax savings or about navigating a new piece of very relevant legislation. The networking element is key to your marketing of the event, this is a major want for most business owners or self employed people as it gives them a chance to promote themselves (Exposure). Couple this with either a collaboration with or you purchasing a fancy place for the event to be held, with free drinks at the bar and you are onto a winner (Ego). Some opinions will be different here and that is fine, events as an offer from a Raise Your Hand perspective need to be a bit more gregarious than usual. Events as an offer, especially for B2B industries, are vast and if you want to try them, the above wouldn't be a bad start. You can see the ego and exposure theory being used again to enhance the offer.

For B2C, you could host a product evening, class or something that gives the prospect value and they leave with knowledge and obviously lots of freebies. You could be a kitchen company, a good event idea would be a cooking class for example. If you are a gym, the event could be a free pilates evening with an expert. There are an abundance of ideas. Events run constantly, events are more of a platform than an offer. The world of events won't change, it's just what you put together in terms of value that does.

ything, leave their office or home and they get the value. This works, but they aren't in front of you and therefore are a prospect that's a bit further behind than a direct conversation. A webinar is also a low-cost method of educating your prospects in an event style format. Raising hands for webinars right now is very, very difficult and the show up rate to said webinars is even worse. This isn't to say it doesn't work; it just needs to be part of a wider strategy and utilize the ego and exposure rules if B2B and emotion and aspiration rules if you are B2C. You can enhance any offering following these rules and webinars are included. You could host a webinar and record it, and this way you are creating great content for your business and it's less of an issue if the show up rate isn't great. Then follow the video content format, asking people whether they would like to see a recording. Webinars can be a great way, with higher show up rate, to engage with your current customer base for further information or to engage an email database. Getting the show up rate is the hard part. The trick here is the volume of invites and following the rules. Collaborate with other businesses too, or influencers. Increase the value of your event to your audience and more people will respond to your raise your hand copy on the various platforms.

I also use Raise Your Hand copy like 'comment #recording and we will send you a copy directly'. This in my last post generated over 1000 comments. This brings 'one thing' theory into your marketing, something you will learn about later on.

Meetings

To build an offer around meetings, you need to first think about why someone would invest their time in you. It has to be in return for value, big value. Typically, meetings are outcomes of a solid Raise Your Hand offer, perhaps the reciprocation you aim for after your giveaway; however, in some circumstances, this can be drafted into a direct offer. Suited for busier people, this does have a lower conversion rate than others but if you hit the correct need, it can be a predictable and consistent offer that you put in front of prospects. Like events or documents you create, having a niche focus to your meeting invite and focusing on a problem the prospect is likely facing will allow for a bigger hand raise uptake than normal meeting requests. This works best in industries where there is a need for your service or product in order for your prospects to complete their product or service. I.e. if you are a manufacturer and you are targeting the construction industry, it is often the case that the prospect will require your product/service (Or one of your competitors) to complete theirs. In this case, it is quite simple to put a request into them focusing on one of the issues they are facing. Common issues could be supply chain, efficiency, timing, pricing, etc. You can develop the copy for your meeting by focusing on one of the issues at hand. This sounds incredibly simple, but you would be surprised how many people send out crap copy about them and get frustrated why the results are not great.

For other industries where the need is more subtle and the market more complicated, a giveaway to raise hands and identify prospects first will be the more efficient route. Alternatively, you could dress the meetings slightly differently, seeing as facetime is the golden egg in Raise Your Hand Marketing. People often use podcasting or interviews to create thought leadership content and build collaboration for their brand. These requests to prospects are nearly always meetings that discuss subject matter relating to the industry. The meeting creates facetime and creates opportunities for relationships to be built. This more subtle meeting approach is applicable in any industry and leads to multiple assets, content, conversation, and reach via the prospect sharing the content to their networks.

Other people's stuff

Your network and industry is teeming with thought leadership, and if you are struggling for content inspiration, you can leverage other people's stuff to create a larger content flow than usual. This used to be called content curation, as you would find an article and put your spin on it to go out online or wherever you placed content. This tactic allowed for lots of content to be made in a short space of time. With Raise Your Hand, you can enhance this strategy by doing a few things. The first would be to ask the person you would like to curate, forming a relationship opportunity and potentially a share from them. Simple yet very effective. The second would be to curate content and then seek out people who engaged prior, that fit your target market and ask them if they have a view on your spin on the topic. This is obviously alongside just posting it, as you want to create interaction.

Be careful not to plagiarize here, it's very easily done and you need to put an honest spin or add credit where it is due. This strategy will allow for low time investment and help you become a news outlet for the industry, which would be a great goal to have.

Collaborative Interviews

Collaborative interviews are another great offer format that creates conversation as well as creates content. You can interview potential customers, industry leaders, or other people that you think would be a great conversation/great piece of content. If you were to ask industry leaders or people you want to do business with for a simple introductory conversation, your results would be minimal. The reason is there is nothing in it for them at this stage, there is no problem being solved, and you are hunting for the one or two that at this point in time are thinking about your service. The interview offer brings in ego and exposure by asking someone to talk about their experience and their story, as well as gain some exposure from you sharing the finished content. What happens during an interview? You have a conversation, probably a very focused one at that where you are asking them questions. Should your questions be built to create great content but also offer you insight into the prospects' needs? Absolutely! Can that be done in a way that creates only positive conversation and is a first-date style question-and-answer session? Absolutely.

The same way that you were asked to think about collaborative content above, the interview or podcast strategy follows the same model.

A beauty product supplier could use this model if they would like to expand their permanent content base, boost engagement with their users as well as talk to fantastic B2B contacts. They want to talk with salon owners with a view of the salon taking the beauty company as a supplier. They ask Salon owners to be interviewed about their stories, experiences and provide tips to up and coming stylists or salons. They raise their hands at a high rate because the offer uses ego and the beauty product supplier offers exposure by promising the edited content will be shared on socials and to email databases. This solves a problem for the salon as they get permanent positive content about their company for free and helps their image or hiring potential. The beauty supplier company creates a positive relationship and can use that conversation and reciprocity to move the relationship forward. How is our salon going to respond to further marketing now they have a relationship with the supplier? Far more positively. The supplier will also generate information from the questions about challenges, mistakes and where the salon wants to go, allowing further tailoring of marketing thereon.

People often think marketing is about selling. Marketing is actually about the information you gather and then how you tailor offerings to that information, knowing your chance of success is far greater. Relationships built early on will allow for more of this and the more conversations you have, the more information you gather. You could build two, three, or four information gathering dates before you propose a buying relationship.

A note on offers

Record as much as you can, collaborate as much as you can, and always build in permission/ask into your offer distribution plan. This is a taste of offers, there will be more to discuss, but you would be here for the next 300 pages assessing them all. Any offer or idea you have, make sure it follows the rules above and be bold in your investment. The bigger the offer, the bigger the value and the more problems you solve, the higher the rate of hands being raised you will achieve. These offers can then be put across all platforms for maximum reach, as remember, the platform doesn't change.

What about freemium, discounts, and memberships, etc.? These would be classed as second dates and will be covered later on.

Examples of offers that aren't as great:

#1 Offering a consultation

Many offers seen in the marketing world are offers of free consultations. A free consultation is something that should be offered when a problem is clear and the prospect has actively mentioned it. Using a consultation as an initial hand raise is not going to generate big results unless you already have a relationship with the prospect.

#2 Discount

Whilst discount can create sales and will do forever more, if you use this to begin with and without prior relationship or planning (by using distribution channels like groups who offer your service en-masse at discount to buy bulk customers) then you will most likely attract price shoppers who are there only for the need you are solving, low cost. Discount is a great tool for buying future relationships and added spend but as an initial offer, it can be dangerous.

#3 Anything related to marriage

This part of the chapter could go on and on, so instead, think about it this way. If your offer is in any way focused at that point on a sale and is more about you than it is about information gathering, the relationship and the future of that relationship, make sure you take a step back and add a further offer that is more wide in value. This will ensure your volume into your second date or marriage proposal is far higher.

Raise Your Hand Garden Corp

Raise Your Hand Gardens Corp has their target market at the ready and knows the level of conversations they need to achieve their goals. They have been thinking about their offers and before they look at what platforms to choose, they have decided that the following will enable them to hit their conversation goals. As they are high ticket B2C, they need to drive conversation flow a little differently and create engaging content:

1. Las Vegas Gardens Of The Week

This strategy is going to be one that creates conversations but also allows RYH Gardens Corp to tackle their content strategy at the same time.

The offer will ask homeowners whether they would like to be interviewed and have a tour of their garden filmed in an effort to be featured on Las Vegas Gardens Of The Week. Ego is used to create exceptional take up and RYH Gardens Corp can use the ask as a big 'wow' to the prospect to initiate a conversation. They send a videographer around to one stunning, high value, garden per week, and film it with the owner talking about their inspiration.

This creates an exceptional relationship opportunity, where RYH Gardens Corp can have easy access to some of the best gardens in the city and probably their biggest client opportunities. Relationship one!

Secondary to this, the content is then posted and due to aspiration, viewers will tune in to see who's got what and the large engagement will allow RYH

Gardens Corp to create further distribution opportunities for their other offers, or inbound enquiries to be on Las Vegas Gardens Of The Week. All videos will have calls to actions and promote conversation. Relationship two!

Finally, the content can be curated in a way that asks the prospect lots of questions and leads to a 'would it be a terrible idea' question around quoting, support for their garden and more. This relationship will allow for RYH Gardens Corp to ask for referrals and get word of mouth flowing due to the amazing content and aspiration smashing offer they have built. Relationship three!

This seems like a lot of work and investment but it doesn't need to be. RYH Gardens Corp wants to be a multi-million dollar company and have to make an impact in their local area. The investment in simple videography and editing is the starting point and this can start simple, gathering in quality and pace as the business grows and is successful.

2. Free Grass Food Kit

RYH Gardens Corp often sells grass food kits or healthy supplements for peoples gardens. These are usually low-cost to the company and a great purchase for prospects. RYH Gardens Corp has decided that each quarter, they will have a new giveaway based around overstock and wanting to help the health of gardens in Las Vegas. They have a form on their site and advertise their offer to everyone with gardens to claim their free gift. Due to this offer being something most of their market needs due to the whole target market that was created having a garden, they can be sure of a high hand raise rate. The form will contain a few questions and, due to the reciprocity, will allow for RYH Gardens Corp to safely create further relationship opportunities and develop the conversation until a clear buying opportunity is raised.

3. Flower Of The Month Club

For their aspirational and garden-loving target market, launching a flower of the month club with a local flower shop brings in collaborative opportunities as well as reciprocity they can use for future marketing. With the flower of the month club, people can sign up to a mailing and blog list by providing their information. The local flower shop partner will allow the member to choose a set of seeds per month from a catalog and a collaborative information pack on the flower and how to care for it. This is an amazing opportunity for them to generate a lot of new relationships too, so they are excited. The flower club is the educational content tool discussed above, and the education is geared towards caring for their gardens and building reciprocity in the form of thank yous for the gifts. This will give RYH Gardens Corp the perfect opportunity to monitor who is engaging with what content, and what the comments are and create tailored proposals.

The above are just some ideas for a business that is being used as an example in this book. You can see how the theory from this book has been used to create their offers. They understand that relationships are key and have taken a step back from marriage proposals and focused on wide market needs. Their offers cater to everyone in their market and they have enough variation that they can be sure there will be uptake for each type of person. The ego type, the hungry deal hunter and the passionate prospects.

14

Copy

Copy! What is copy?

Well copy is very simply how you put your offers in front of the people you want to talk to. Different platforms require different levels of copy so for this chapter, you are going to focus simply on the theory of copy and some key tips. After this, you will dive into platforms and finish off with a chapter on adapting copy to different platforms.

There are a few rules which need to be followed and some interesting psychology that can be brought in here. Remember, you are looking for self identification from prospects, which triggers our law of reciprocity and allows them to feel in control. This is vitally important. For all direct communication platforms, this must be done by asking them if they want the offer, not by telling them. Seeking permission from them is vitally powerful and whilst this is harder in more spend driven campaigns like advertising, it can be done. We have included a few re-writes that will help you visualize this. WIIFM, the 'what's in it for me' methodology you discussed in prior chapters will also play into your development.

Typically, negativity plays an interesting part in your copy preparation. Adding the use of scarcity and only, which are in theory negative language as well as focusing on pain areas, allows us to create more need. You are not selling here, so none of this copy will be that intense; however it does have to get our offer across clearly, exclusively and with a time frame. An example Raise Your Hand offer for a social media post/ad could be the following for example:

The business is a music equipment business and wants to build relationships with budding musicians, especially guitar players which is where a large investment in stock is going in the next 6 months.

"Calling all guitarists! We have stock of the new Ernie Ball X Strings for electric guitar and you would like to give 10 guitar players here a few free sets in order to get an expert opinion for our blog! First come first served, just send us a DM or write 'ernie' below on the post before the weekend and our team will be in touch"

What did this copy do?

1. It is highly clear to our target market and brings a brand the guitarists know and trust into the offer.

2. It gives exclusivity in the sense there are only 10 sets available.

3. It gives a time frame in that the business needs this completed by the following weekend.

A bonus is that the guitar shop will probably end up with some great content coming out of it too for their blog and some fantastic relationship conversations.

Asking:

By far, the most powerful way of enticing someone to raise their hand is simply asking them if they would like your offer. Most people will brush aside exclamatory campaigns and miss them. Especially the younger audience, who have an evolved ad-blocker ingrained into their minds and automatically miss most ads. Did you know that ads are predominantly on the right hand side of the screen and most millennials have actually developed a skill that blocks this out automatically?

This 'ask' element of this section is really very simple and should be built into your copy tests. Adding a 'We have seen this problem and have a solution, I'd like to send it over to you, would that be ok?' has a very strong success rate. Granted, if you can get in front of the person to make your 'ask', then the results will be even better, digitally or physically.

Permission:

Permission is an unbelievably powerful tool that should be used either in copy or in the initial conversation. By asking permission, you are creating a sense of control for the prospect, allowing them to remain in control. Using even something as simple as 'with your permission, I would like to give you a call' takes the pressure off a marriage proposal. This worked well back in 2013-15, but as you have seen, the world is a different place. Now you need to use your new conversation-driving offers and combine this with a copy that follows permission and asking questions to make sure your offer gets through.

Your call to action

The golden rule for any 'call to action' is simplicity. The key here is that if you ask the prospect to do too much, your conversation rate will drop drastically. Your job is to handhold the soon-to-be prospect through the process and do as much of it as possible to make sure they complete their hand raise. It is not uncommon for fantastic strategies with well-executed plans crumble due to over complicated sign up processes for the offer. This will just create the dreaded 'this doesn't work' reaction to the strategy when there could be a very simple fix. These things need to be determined for your industry, but it is suggested that you provide your prospect with just one or two things to do in order to redeem the offer you have provided. A simple task like booking a discussion for example, has wildly swinging effects depending on the level of complication and how much you ask your prospect to do.

At Avalanche we deal with upwards of 10,000 conversation hand raises per month. An example of using permission is below:

We work with a consultancy firm to develop relationships as well as providing us with a strong content strategy simultaneously with our interview series. When a prospect agrees to get involved, there is typically a 65-70% booking rate from hand raised to interview actually being booked. This is achieved through us booking it for the prospect and making sure the prospect simply has to provide us with a confirmation of date. Initially, you would provide a calendar link to the prospect and ask them to complete the booking themselves and the rate of completion? Around 30%. This is a stark difference that showcases the sensitivity of prospects at this stage. They are not ready to commit effort to go out of their way at this stage, you have solved a small problem by offering exposure for them but they need to be guided through the process with us in control. Being in control of each stage, as discussed earlier in the book, will allow for the predictability and consistency elements of Raise Your Hand marketing to occur. Without these, it will not be anywhere as good as it could be.

The level of what you can ask your prospect to complete during the CTA phase of the hand raising process is going to be dependent on the size of your offer and the problem at hand. This will be easier to do for transactional offers but if you are a B2B or long sales cycle organization then you need to be prepared to put the work in and hold the hand of your prospect, nurturing them through each stage and probably, do a lot of following up.

In a study conducted across all of the data Avalanche has collected in the last 8 years, it was found that if a prospect who has raised their hand is asked to do more than one simple action the actual conversation rate dropped by over 40%. That is a scary difference and something to be noted as you pull together your copy and begin to understand what will happen when someone engages with your offer.

A few examples of simple call to actions could be 'Comment #recording below', 'Just respond with 'interested'', 'If you are interested, simply provide your phone number and one of the team will call'. All of these ask the prospect to do something simple. If you have a big ticket item, like a $500 giveaway, you can ask for more information. The most important lesson here is to make it simple and judge the information you want based on the value of your offer. If it is a simple ebook offer, ask for one click or word as a response. If it is a $500 coffee machine or something like the Las Vegas Gardens Of The Week, ask for a little more information. Every industry and offer will be different, so you will need to monitor this and tweak your call to action to suit. If there is a high rate of hands being raised and low actual conversation, the problem is likely with your call to action rather than your offer.

I ran an offer with a client who had a 50% conversation rate after the hand was raised. This showed us that the offer was very strong but the call to action was either not flexible enough for different preferred platforms of communication (Some people like forms, some people like a call). Changes made to these follow up methods and increasing the simplicity of the call to action increased that to 80% quickly. There will always be some drop off but do not give up at the first hurdle. Follow up five or six times before you move them to the 'not interested' pile.

The follow up when seeking to book in conversations or deliver offers is vital and make sure you are diligent, use the platforms at your disposal and be persistent. You know the person wants it, so make sure you get it in front of them.

Remember though, you are looking for more hand raises than you can handle so you can bring exclusivity into the conversation. This brings us on to the word 'only'...

Only - Scarcity Theory

Humans are animals of exclusivity. This ties in our ego, emotion, aspiration, and exposure marketing tactics with basic human psychology. How much do you see exclusivity playing a part of the brands marketing across social media, across TV, or pretty much across any other team media outlet you see on a day-to-day basis? It is pretty much all of them right? Exclusivity in terms of your customer base has been discussed before and links well with the limiting of how many of your offers are being made available ever each month or week. This required exclusivity can actually be built in a way that helps your copy and increases your conversation rate. If you only had eight potential sale spots this month in my business, for example, you could build that into your marketing into my conversations. By creating exclusivity or at least leveraging actual requirements for exclusivity, you can lean on one of the most standard and frequent needs of the human race. This is the need to fit in and to be involved, which in turn creates one of the most powerful sales opportunities for businesses to lean on and leverage in order to grow.

In 2022 there was a crazy example of this in the global watch market. Swiss watchmakers, such as Rolex or Patek Philippe, Richard Mille, and others, have a very sophisticated and very public exclusivity arrangement with their customers. These watchmakers agree to make a very small number of the pieces yet market as if everyone can have access. This is because they are engineering exclusivity in the market by creating a product at a semi reasonable price and then marketing it as uber luxury and something that everyone needs, whilst only having a set number of pieces on the market creates a massive exclusivity around their product. The people who are lucky enough to buy them are forever attached to their brand because they see amazing marketing and celebrities wearing their watches, making them feel like a celebrity (emotion & aspiration). This engineered exclusivity creates a secondhand market for products, at a price far higher than Rolex would sell their watches for. This gap in price from retail to aftermarket ensures that a retail price Rolex will never go unsold. The continuous cycle of this low production amount versus huge aspiration for products will mean that Rolex can increase their prices every single year at a higher rate than their production costs increase. This example, it's so widely public, and so widely bought into by said public that it is a great example of exclusivity marketing for the word only. These watchmakers have bought lifetime customers and raving fans to a level unseen in any other market other than high fashion.

Unlike Rolex, for example, you are probably going to be marketing from scratch and do not have the level of trust Rolex carries. Your offers and communication will need to be more basic and more focused on developing that trust. It doesn't mean that as the relationship develops and the higher ticket offers are used, these shouldn't be exclusive, at least in your copy, to ignite the aspirational and exclusivity psychology talked about in this chapter. Use your customer onboarding figures from part one that you know will create exceptional delivery but grow your business. Raise as many hands as possible for a limited number spaces on your next offer, all inline with your conversation target. Your marketing is going to be the whole target market, lot's of hands will be raised but as the baker found out, you can't accept them all into conversation or delivery of the offer. If you have 50 cakes to giveaway, you can't give away 60. You build in the exclusivity and delivery capabilities into your copy using the word 'only'...

'Only' is one of the greatest words in marketing copy. In your own use of the word, there will actually be some truth to said 'only' statement, the copy is derived from the level of volume you can handle that retains quality of delivery. This word would be brought in like, 'We are giving away just 50 x 1lb bags of grass feed! Each lb is valued at $40, and all you need to do is click on the link and lead your details. One of our team will then ship the food for delivery in the next 3-5 business days.' This copy brings in exclusivity by using a limit to the offer, creating a sense of urgency. Due to the offer distribution potential, meaning there are far more people who would like this offer than it is available.

Aspiration comes back into play when thinking about the word 'only'. Aspiration works by showcasing products and services that people would really like that they feel may be slightly out of current reach or may make them feel better or feel like they are doing better than they currently are. Aspiration is a very positive tool that is used every day by brands all over the world. It can, however, be used negatively, as you will have seen in countless ads like get-rich-quick schemes or courses that will make you rich in 22 days for example. The key with using aspiration properly is to focus on what you can provide and what needs you can solve. If you were to walk into a bar and order a pint of beer, yet the barman only gave you a half pint, how often would you drink at that bar? On the flip side, if the barman gave you the full pint, you'd enjoy it and be happy, but a pint with a free shot as well? You love this bar. This analogy has been made to show you the difference between over promising and under delivery. It is easy to write the world's greatest copy, heck, you could write an ad tomorrow offering $5000 to anyone that clicked on it. You likely wouldn't be able to fulfill your ad but you would get people raising their hands. All this will do is turn people off, so make sure that when you are pulling together your offer and copy, you underpromise and overdeliver and at least serve a full pint every time.

You can use exclusivity and aspiration within your target, offer, and copy to create exceptional strategies that will raise the hands of your potential customers. This will also create long-term exclusivity around your brand and eventually, if done right, create more opportunities than there are spots available.

Now, the question will be placed here about type of business and/or size of market but in theory the above works exactly the same. Whether you are a small business with a target audience of only 1000 in your geographical area and you need only 30 new customers per year or whether you are Rolex with 500,000 potential customers per year, it should, in theory, be easier for the smaller business and far less costly. If you remember, with Raise Your Hand marketing, you are looking to market to the 90%. You leave your competitors to market to the 10%. This is the 10% of a target market that wants to buy right now, and you raise their hands without competition with the 90% of suspects who just want a conversation right now. If you can build exclusivity and the word only into our plan around targeting this 90%. The number of conversations you will be having compared to our competitors and the aspiration you build due to the volume will be incredible.

So how do you build scarcity, only an aspiration, into our marketing? First of all, you need to be careful not to overdo it. Overdoing it At an early stage could be detrimental, especially as you are in the beginning giving rather than getting. The initial use of the word only within our Marketing will be subtle and built over time as you begin having further sales conversations and customers begin moving up the ladder of loyalty. Its typical use of the word only at the giving stage will be, for example, "you only have one copy of this book available", what this does is showcase that you have a very small number of our give available. In theory, this is true because you do not have unlimited gifts available otherwise you would not actually be able to run a business, so building an element of truth into this will make sure that the copy is not too unrealistic that it creates detriment and looks too over the top at this stage. My recommendation is to keep your numbers low. For example, don't say you have 10,000 of these available as the urgency and only nature of that number is probably too high. You do want to create urgency and that is the next word as part of our scarcity mindset conversation.

Conversation around the only and scarcity mindset has given us what to think about when drafting the copy of an offer. These are aspiration only, exclusivity and finally urgency. Urgency should be your way of pulling together copy, as this is really what only does. You build an offer that gives your customers what they need or want right now, asking them to identify themselves. The conversation will discuss how there are only a certain number of said offers available. This will create urgency and you can embellish this by simply putting a time limit on the offer itself. So practice this and make sure to test and measure various numbers of examples in order to get the best version of it.

Calendar Links!

You may believe that a calendar link is a simple solution, but it isn't. You are making the prospect think, and they do not want to think. If there is one call to action or copy piece of advice you should take away from this book, it is to make sure you do the work for the prospect when they are accepting their offer and setting up your reciprocated conversation. If the prospect says yes to a conversation or accepts your offer and this offer requires a call or meeting, do not provide your calendar link. Instead, offer times available, preferably two, and ask them which one suits. You can also ask them if they would prefer a phone call to schedule the appointment, they just need to respond with their number. They will remember you!

There are various forms of platform that the copy theory learned in this chapter can be applied to. In the next chapter, you will learn about these and how they work. After this, a few examples will be provided by Raise Your Hand Gardens Corp to illustrate how the theory can be applied to each platform.

15

Platforms & Distribution

Now you have your target, offer and copy clearly defined, and following the Raise Your Hand rules, you can put the final piece of the puzzle in place by choosing platforms to distribute your offer to your target market effectively. The goal of this chapter is to examine how traditional marketing platforms and well thought through offers can see dramatic increases in conversation rates and growth. If you combine your offers with these platforms, adapt the copy, and follow the rules, you will see success. With Raise Your Hand marketing, you should be able to see 5 or 6 multiple gains in engagement. This is due to the fact you have thought your offer through well and know there is a good chance people will want this now rather than later. You should be able to make your marketing more enjoyable, easier to manage, and 100% better at improving the morale of your marketing team. Whilst this chapter will be predominantly about platforms, i.e how you would use social media with Raise Your Hand marketing, there will be applications to your initial hand raise as well as your continued hand raises as you develop the relationship. Once you understand how your target, offer and copy matches with each platform works, examine how you use each platform to develop a strong, measurable plan for the first purchase, the second purchase, and finally, strategies that will build lifetime value during the plan development.

Social Media

A large portion of marketing strategies revolve around social media. It's become a phenomenon none of us could have imagined but in reality, it makes so much sense. Social media connects people quickly, old and new and allows a platform for the one thing that overpowers all in the world of marketing... Ego. One of the most egotistical places if not the most egotistical place on earth is social media. It's rife with aspiration, people oversharing, and frankly, is the perfect place to reach nearly everyone you want to speak to. How you use social media will differ from business to business. Whether it's with influencers (ego) that reach tens of millions of people all the way to simple communication strategies with small business-to-business markets, social media is the one platform recommended for all businesses to use. In December of 2023, a quarter of the earth's population logged onto Meta's platforms Instagram & Facebook, a quarter of the earth's population!

Social media can be a waste of money if you continue to propose on the first date, so it's up to you whether you change or not. There are different types of uses for social media as a platform, and these are the following:

Message Responses Campaigns

For social media, you can utilize direct messaging as a platform to have a conversation and in response to your 'Raise Your Hand' offer. By using the call to action 'DM us' (direct message) in your copy, you can easily initiate a conversation with the prospect, especially if your offer is of high value. You could automate your response, but it is recommended that you first try manual communication. This allows you to test and measure different questions and personalize the response. You found out in prior chapters that the work load switches to nurturing from hunting, this is an example of nurturing. Your offer should be strong enough that your DM's become crowded and this is the perfect opportunity to learn. You should try to leverage the conversation for maximum engagement and maximum information. In the eclair story, the prospect DM'd the bakery to receive information about the free eclair offer. The secondary level of this conversation was asking a few more questions in order for the bakery to give a larger offer and to raise the prospects hand again, furthering the relationship towards a buying a lifetime customer. By wowing the customer on their first physical interaction, the bakery will have a great opportunity to win their business. The information gained in the messaging conversation will allow them to do this. Using a simple freebie, the bakery developed knowledge of the customer and provided a stellar, seemingly spontaneous experience, establishing the bakery as a provider of outstanding service. Asking questions that are aimed at buying lifetime customers will ensure that your DMs aren't wasted.

To map out your use of this platform, become clear on your initial offer and copy, make sure it's crunchy enough to ensure prospects self-identify as interested and then make it very easy for them to raise their hand. A simple DM can usually happen with one click, from the post or ad. Freebies given away by DM's work for any business and product, however, business-to-consumer companies generally see more volume on social media channels like Facebook and Instagram. Business-to-business companies generally have less volume on social media so correct target audience growth needs to be the priority. Revert back to the book Oversubscribed about becoming 'famous' within a small group of highly engaged people as this will showcase in detail what that actually means. Social media caters for half of the globe's population, meaning no matter the customer, they are on the platforms. For some industries, it is just harder to direct campaigns at them right away. In the case of a B2B organization struggling to reach the right people with its ads, starting by building your audience is the best first step. You can do this via Raise Your Hand marketing too by running very low-cost social media ads with hand raises highly specific to your audience. Those that click and engage should be within your target market and although it will likely be low volume, you can then choose to run the ads focused on the type of person who has clicked, therefore generating a much more targeted audience.

It is important to plan out the conversation mapping. The first date is the initial conversation, so what is the second date? You should increase your offer on the second date from the DM to generate more information.

As an example, if I were a clothing company asking for a direct message regarding a voucher offer, I could increase the voucher during the conversation to gain useful information. I could use this information to wow my customer on their use of the voucher i.e. understanding their favorite style, piece of clothing, etc. When they come in store or even if they are online, I could provide them with a free item based on their answers to my questions. This is work, but don't balk at that. You are buying lifetime customers so the investment of time is worth it. A prospect who has been impressed has a great chance of becoming a member and advocate quickly if their buying and quality experience is upheld.

Community Engagement Campaigns

Raise Your Hand marketing is a great tool for community engagement. What this means is the liking, commenting, and sharing of your posts for greater organic reach. Organic reach means the number of people that see your social media post without having to put ad spend behind it. Increasing your community engagement will ensure that the social media engines kicks in and deliver more reach, in a compounding improvement that will maximize the number of people that see your posts. Community engagement can also be a fantastic way for prospects to identify themselves and for you to enter into conversations. Twitter is a great conversation tool, and big brands are engaging with their communities more and more out of the blue. This kicks up lots of shares, likes and even media attention if it's that uncommon and you have enough reach. You want people to be talking about you, waiting for that next post and attached to your brand. Social media gives you the ability to do that. If you see prospects engaging with your post, it can be a great idea to reach out to them to further along the conversation.

Engagement is a hand raise, usually happening when the company provides value to the prospect. Whilst a basic level of hand raise, it does show who is identifying, and again, the platforms have the ability to target your ads at those who engage with your posts. This is why you should be highly active with your content and be seeking engagement. Due to personal use of the platform, sharing emotional stories and aspirational ones too, you know this is something everyone likes to see and is ingrained into their psychology, so by using it, you will drive more engagement. The interesting thing about this is you could play it in two ways; either in an offer format, where you bring our offer and copy into a mass focused post i.e. "If you would like to redeem offer x, just comment 'yes please' below this post!" which will drive comments and engagement on your post, therefore yielding more and more in regards to reach, the more likes and comments the post receives. Alternatively, you could use simple hand raising posts for pure community engagement such as polls, competitions, and other formats of getting your suspect involved can lead to subtle showcases of who may be interested and who may not. You could set some rules for your marketing manager to follow, such as if people engage 3-4 times on your posts, but they are not yet a customer, then they would be directly messaged with an offer exclusive to them for being a fantastic engager. This makes for a great conversation starter. A more aggressive approach would be to thank everyone who engages. This should be done with caution to not be too overpowering. However, it is a great way to boost engagement and once you have nailed it, you can begin to enhance your posts with a budget for greater reach.

Furthering on from community engagement, community development is growing your follower base on social media. You don't need to be a global sensation and viral sensation to generate a lot of business; you just need to be famous to 5000-10000 people, according to Oversubscribed by Daniel Priestly. Quality is more important than quantity when it comes to using social media, as much of the quantity is fake or done by people engaging with your posts for attention. You may not get tens of thousands of followers by targeting market-driven community development, but you will develop the right type of followers.

By using Raise Your Hand marketing, you can develop your community on social media in a few significant ways. If you raise the hands of other businesses with a similar following to yours, you can generate a collaboration with them. This will result in them sharing whatever you produce together. This is in theory influencer marketing. A simple definition of influencer marketing is to harness the influence of another person or company. For small businesses, this is often known as a host beneficiary, where another business allows you access to their customer/reader base in exchange for either the same type of promotion or a paid placement on or it can be a paid placement. Here, you could simply reach out to your best 5 customers who have similar target markets as you and ask them to share your offer. In order to redeem their free gift, people need to follow both parties or simply make sure they follow both parties.

In the last few years, this method continues to gain strength have used this method to gain tens of thousands of followers, and good ones at that, people you know who are interested in our product or service.

Does your target market have any influencers with large engagement? Influencers are often thought of as famous individuals. There is no need for them to be super famous consumer names for it to work. Are there any business owners with a lot of clouts you could work with? In almost every industry and location, there are micro-influencers. A hair salon once found a few girls with 3000-4000 followers. They were small, but with some content created in return for free services, the salon created a permanent content asset and gained a healthy following. The power of social media, emotion, and aspiration are at your fingertips, as well as half of the world. You can often create permanent content and lead flow simultaneously, saving time and money in the long run while attracting new customers.

Business to business use of social media

Using social media for business-to-business companies is easier than ever and social media becomes more of a communication platform. Using social as a tool in this way is an easy way to control how you generate new prospects consistently. Business-to-consumer companies can work with direct communication, but you have to be careful not to invade too much into someone's personal life and damage your brand. You should love direct messaging campaigns because they allow you to test different targets, offers, and copies without spending a fortune. It is not uncommon for business to business advertising to be rife with bots, low engagement, and low hand raises. A strong direct messaging campaign on LinkedIn, for example, should be a core part of your marketing plan. In the previous chapter, you thought about something our potential customers may need right now in order to get their hands raised. Direct messaging is simply directly asking them if they would like to receive what you have created. By asking someone whether they want something you have developed (and it follows the rule) you can be pretty sure that there will be some take up. Once you have a conversation rate, you can build improvements into it in order to generate stronger conversion rates and measure your steps as you develop the relationship with the prospect.

LinkedIn is the best tool for this when wanting to cultivate new business relationships. LinkedIn is a digital networking platform, and people spent years developing knowledge and strategies around how to use the platform for maximum results. It isn't rocket science; it just comes down to how good your offer is and the needs it solves. You don't need to be a marketing guru to send messages to people, right? The most important thing with LinkedIn is to NOT be lazy with your approach. Due to the thousands of people at your fingertips, it can be very easy to just blast out a bunch of rubbish. The problem with this, like cold calling for marriage proposals or other traditional marketing platforms used in this way, is you will probably get a conversion rate. A conversion rate on a flawed offer is one of the most common things in marketing and one of the reasons there are so many rabbit holes you need to stay out of. This is just like asking someone to marry you on the first date and they say yes. It happens rarely, but when it does, there is a lot of noise and a bunch of other people try to do it and fail. The same goes for marketing. Some bright spark messages 100 people with a super direct salesy message and one person just so happens to be in need right now for their product or service. The chances are, it probably won't be a lifetime relationship.

In order to create sustainability, the Raise Your Hand technique must be used because the above is not predictable or sustainable. Using the same offer & copy techniques you have used for posts, you can create something that you can use on LinkedIn to create an initial conversation. The same theory would work for any of the social media platforms in regard to direct messaging suspects.

As an example, a law firm only sometimes engages in direct marketing. By using this method, they can develop a simple offer that provides value to prospects without having to sell them anything. It's usually some kind of tip sheet. An example would be an employment lawyer who has developed a document for executives titled 'An executive's guide to employment law'. The fact that law is a very front-of-mind business and that not everyone needs a lawyer on a regular basis means marketing needs to focus on providing value consistently to prospects. This value acts as a tool to bring the law firm front of mind. When the prospect then thinks of needing a lawyer, there is a much larger chance they will think of the law firm sending them lots of valuable information and whom they have had a personal interaction with.

Another example would be a consultant who wants to talk with CEOs. While directly messaging CEOs for a call will yield some sort of result, rarely, it will not yield the level of prospects that will allow them to supercharge your conversations and predict growth. The consultant could create a lead magnet for the CEO, inviting them to an interview to discuss their business and the future of their industry/your industry or some sort of event where they can gain/speak. There have even been instances where boxes at football games are rented and the CEO is invited to the game, this is simply a raise your hand offer that is so great in size, the CEO will provide a huge reciprocal response and spend time with the person inviting them. Despite being expensive, it does lead to a lot of hands being raised! These ideas should give you some thought, as they can be used in any business-to-business industry. They focus on right now and solve an imminent need.

Direct messaging should be included in your marketing plan at a minimum if you are a business-to-business company. You can allocate time and develop a low-cost, scalable conversation generation tool with this controllable strategy. Although it is a very manual process, this strategy as a whole with the correct target, offer, copy, and a little consistency does work. Do not be put off by the hard work. Leverage and automation will come. First use manual strategies to drive this forward.

A suggestion would be to place 5 hours per week of your team's time to reach out directly and ask potential prospects if they would like your offer. If it is a low response, up your offer value or change the problem you solve. Alternatively, if your offer gets a lot of interest but little follow through in terms of conversation, think about your copy, your call to action and how you communicate. You can choose how many messages you want to send or how many connection requests you want to make, for instance. Don't worry too much about the conversation numbers too early on. It''s very hard to predict these until you have tried it. Rather than focusing on the outcome, start with the process. It would be possible for someone to send around 200 requests and around 50 messages on LinkedIn or over 100 messages on Instagram in 5 hours per week.

Social Media Advertising

Advertising on social media is typically split into two types. You have genuine ads, which can be by often on their own and not attached to the post feed of the platform, and you have promoted posts which is generally a poster has done well or the ad done as an actual social media post that then has a budget behind it to reach more people. Advertisement social media is an extremely powerful way to leverage Raise Your Hand offers and enhance your reach. The sheer volume in reach available to you is massive and if you can get the right target, offer and copy, you can make sure that as a tool to raise hands, social advertising is almost second to nothing else when it comes to size and cost. The opportunities to generate relationships and further conversation are massive. The best type of business this can be used for is a business-to-consumer brand but it can be part of your plan, the offer will just need to be crunchy and cut through the busy noise of business peoples lives when they're at work. The reason it works so well for consumer-driven companies is because social media currently has over a quarter of the planet's population actively logging in each month and almost half owning an account. Over 1.6 billion people login to Facebook and over 500 million people into Instagram every single day.

Good results on Facebook for Instagram when attempting to raise hands and initiate relationships will depend again on the offer. You have seen examples throughout this book of bakeries and hair salons, simple businesses where the offer is very much wanted by the prospect and low cost to the business. You should try to make sure that your business follows that process and find something again that is low cost and high value in order to generate as many hand raises as possible. The first steps to building an advertisement campaign is obviously to make sure that our offer and copy is correct, then to make sure that you are using the correct ad tool. Do you want message responses? Do you want to collect your website? Do you want followers? These are all questions you need to ask her to determine what type of add to use. With any advertisement there should be an AB test system put in place to make sure that you are not putting your eggs in one basket. There's a long old alphabet there and you shouldn't just stop at B. Other than that, social media advertising isn't complicated.

I own a few hair salons and we used to give away 400 free blow drys a month with social media ads. The ad was nothing special, it was the offer that drove bookings.

Telemarketing (Phone marketing)

Telemarketing is a traditional platform used by businesses all around the world still today. Full stop, it is one of the original time-based, controllable strategies where more volume nearly always meant results. Telemarketing has been glamorized by movies, the grind and hustle culture you live in today but it can be one of the most soul-destroying tactics known to any marketing person. It is one of the lowest engagement traditional strategies in marketing today, yet it is still widely used globally. Why? Because when the conversations do happen, they lead to relationships. Telemarketing is also becoming frowned upon in many businesses due to the work at takes and due to this automation culture you live in, pushing funnels in your faces every single day with the promise of a passive flow of clients without lifting a finger. Just like passive income, it doesn't really become passive until you're quite wealthy, and even then a large portion of your income will still require elements of work. It is uncommon to come across a business that does not have to work on relationships and could not benefit from doubling or tripling the number of conversations that they're having on a weekly or monthly basis. If you harness this correctly, telemarketing can be one of the most powerful Raise Your Hand platforms in this book. This again is more so for business-to-business companies over business-to-consumer as it is time-based and typically consumer data is not available for marketing use unless pre-agreed.

The problem faced by any telemarketing person is the fact they are intruding on someone's day unannounced. There is generally very little permission involved. Raise Your Hand marketing techniques should mean that your telemarketing is much more widely accepted, if you are going cold, because you are simply calling to ask them whether they want something, for free, that they need right now.

At ActionCOACH, we often giveaway books as simple hand raises and the response rate goes from less than 1% to more like 15%. As a follow up, we may drop the book off in person to initiate a conversation and invite the prospect to an event, or offer a referral as a way to cement a relationship and form the law of reciprocity. This simple call to ask whether someone is interested in receiving our value turns into a full funnel of relationship building.

A way to introduce a layer of subconscious permission or at least a touch point prior to your call is the use of mail either physical mail or emailing ahead to let them know that you will be calling and what the call may be about.

Mail/Lumpy Mail (Direct Mail Campaigns)

Lumpy mail is used more as an initial touch point to initiate familiarity with your brand, that is the prequel to the true conversation starter in the form of ads, direct contact or networking. It's a conversation starter that when you ask someone if they saw it (already knowing it was sent to them), they positively acknowledge and it develops a layer of trust. If you want highly measurable results that really matter, for any type of mail, have an extremely clear and redeemable offer within that may carry a bit of physical weight.

Lumpy mail is the act of sending letters to prospects that have something in them to make them stand out from all of the other letters that the prospect has received. The term lumpy comes from the fact the letter usually has a lump in it, as simple as that. Again like any strategy, this only works with a strong follow up and a first date mentality. If you go into it thinking you are going to generate very qualified leads, this will be a rare occurrence. What is good about this strategy is that there is a high chance of the prospect opening the mail and receiving your gift therefore it is often used. It is very memorable! Then, in your further communications or future interactions with the prospect, you can leverage this for acknowledgments and use it to enhance the trusting relationship you are building.

An example of this again would be ActionCOACH in the UK. They often send a scratch lotto card with a $1 cost with a potential win of $100,000 on it, or is a lucky dip to the major lotto draw. This is hilarious but also highly effective because, well, who isn't going to remember the company that sent them a chance to become a millionaire? The coaches then communicate and lead on this gift as part of the conversation and it makes presenting their offer, which is still a hand raise driving offer at this stage, far more accepted.

What could you send that includes a bit of a lump?

Content Driven Platforms:

The following strategies are content driven elements and there should be a budget of time/money towards building and maintaining them.

Your Website

Your website is receiving traffic, or should be, and therefore you need to make sure our site calls to actions are prime for raising hands. Many people do not have enough calls to action on their website. Your website should be a hand raising machine. There should be stacks of opportunities and need-solutions on their prime and ready for your newly increased traffic. As with any offer and copy, which will be on your website's calls to action, you need to solve a need our visitor has right now. The outcome of this could simply be more site time, hitting correct pages, or gaining their information/redeeming a conversational offer. To make this simple for now, as you are already going to be testing out various new offers and copy, create a page or element of the relevant pages with the same offer and copy as in your hand raises for your ads pointing to your site and the strategies where you will be talking to people in person. The more professional and well thought out it all looks, the higher the rate of trust and the higher chance of a better engagement.

Your Website - SEO

This section was extremely interesting to dive into and I drafted in Laura Kraman, who has spent decades working as SEO director for major corporations and is currently the SEO Director for Deloitte, to help me provide you with some insight into how SEO can be used for Raise Your Hand marketing but also give you 3 or 4 absolutely vital and easy to implement tools that will improve your ranking and get more people seeing your new wonderful target, offer and copy.

SEO, or search engine optimization is a distribution that is difficult to include a target offer, copy on in simple terms. It is more the home for your offer and copy, with your targeting built into the copy via key words and rank building with the search engines. Using the correct language and building layers into your website makes sure it is seen and communicated properly, so Google will make sure that your progress compounds. Whilst a marketing plan and the strategies you develop within are relatively short term measurement points, it is highly recommended having some time and effort put into SEO so that as your traffic grows with your conversation budget, the site grows also.

Raise Your Hand Marketing is an attraction tool and works perfectly with SEO. Your proactive marketing is a giving machine that creates conversation and engagement that compounds in the long term. SEO is exactly the same. It takes effort and consistency now that will pay huge dividends in the long run and you do not need to be an expert to complete the suggestions coming up next.

The most important things google looks for:

Google is just a machine. It simply looks for questions and answers throughout so it can match up its information and be as efficient as possible. It wants the best for its users, therefore when someone asks a question, it will take the most efficient route there. Typically that means location, key word and whether or not the site it's looking to send the person too has enough of those 'answer' nodes, as well as being highly efficient, to warrant the spot. The most efficient and most node matching sites will filter to the top and in rank order of this will go down the pages of Google. It is as simple as that.

If your site is not ranked as high as you want, it is due to you not performing well enough in the areas you want to be ranked in. In layman's terms, you haven't put enough answers to your potential visitors' questions and your sites are not set up in the right way. Remember Marcus Sheridan? HIs book They Ask, You Answer is pretty much a manual on how to develop a huge net and work simultaneously with google and other search engines.

The bits you can do:

On Page SEO/Content

On page SEO/Content is about how your page's content reads. There are a few key points to think about here. One of them is to use something called back linking. This is a link behind a word that will actually hyperlink to another page on the site, answering google's machine questions. If you look at your current pages and you are stuck for backlink blogs, just read the content and pick some words you think a blog could be written about.

For example, on an agency site, every time Raise Your Hand marketing is mentioned in a service page, this would link back to our theory post on Raise Your Hand marketing. The same could be for anything. This is a controllable tool you can do as much as you want.

First, take a look at what keywords are needed for the section you are writing about. You can do this by heading to Google's keyword planner. For example, if you are a kitchen manufacturer and you were writing about appliances, you would want to look for keywords people search for when looking at appliances. Re-write your paragraph but add as many keywords in as you can. Once you are done, stick this into word tune or another AI tool that will help you re-write things in a digestible format. These apps mean you don't need to be a great writer, you just need to get your ideas down on paper. The apps will correctly format and grammatically correct your work so when you are done, your paragraph sounds stellar.

Your content needs to be answer driven and focus on the conversation/finding need. Pre-think about the questions people have, write about them and create the needed hand raises for those issues. This way google will send traffic to you and you will retain the traffic, turning it into conversation and business.

Interactive Material/Tools

Google loves interactive tools on your site. You can find these everywhere and there are very intelligent people that have built tools for you to use that are perfect for hand raising. Things like calculators, tests, games, videos, and interactive experiences allow for google to see that the person they are sending to you is going to be looked after. If you run a search for ideas around this in your industry, a bunch of tools will show up for you.

There is no excuse for not having video FAQ's done for your business or other interactive tools that answer questions. If you are going to create one asset out of this, do that!

Blog

Every site needs a blog. Without a blog, it is very difficult for Google to see you as a question answering place to send their traffic and queries they receive. The best thing you can do to start a blog is begin by writing a very large statement piece about your industry as a whole and how the business fits into the industry, your story, and the elements of the industry that you perform in. This should give you blogging categories and lots of ideas for content to begin developing a consistent blog, as well as a place that will fire off links to all your other pages, offers, and blogs to increase retention. It should be around 4000 words. After this, one blog every few weeks on one of the categories in question will suffice back linked to the main blog and other pages relevant on your site. Each blog should have a Raise Your Hand offer in it. The blogs are permanent content, meaning they actually build visibility over time instead of diminish like most social media posts, so make sure you have a gift or conversation engagement point at the end of your blog.

An example blog with this sort of power is with a decorating contractor called Wall 2 Wall Decorating in the UK. The owner isn't a web guru, he's a decorator, but he wrote a blog on how to choose the correct paint that gets 20,000 hits a month on his site. It's a simple blog, but it answers an obviously needed question. For a small decorator, this is huge and it initially created 20 x their monthly web traffic over night.

The bits you need to ask someone to do (Unless you're a site and google wizz):

Areas you need to ask for help on and to create a list for completion that will increase your performance technically are:

- Meta Tags & Meta Descriptions
- Correct Google Search Console submissions
- Make sure your sitemap is correct

To conclude, this very short introduction into SEO set up so that your site is as powerful as it should be for the increased traffic Raise Your Hand marketing will bring is just that, very short. Put the three key areas mentioned into place and you will be night and day in a better position. Ask for help on the latter areas. Be unique, be consistent and be patient!

Email Marketing

Getting the prospects' email address and having a good CRM system to track it is vital. There is no use generating all of this wonderful information if there is no place to track it and use it. It will allow you to test and measure email marketing properly. Email marketing has been in and out of popularity for the last 3 decades. Initially, people new to the internet were wildly willing to buy things from email marketing, which then ended up being saturated, as any strategy does in the long run when it is full of marriage proposals, price competition arises and spam blockers are invented. Email is still up there as one of the largest level of professional communication platforms out there. It is very, very rare that anyone is building relationships or using Raise Your Hand offers and copies in their email, asking the prospect to do something in return for value that they need right now. Email marketing should be split into stages:

1. **List building & initial touch points:** The best lists are built by value and if you are expecting to just buy data and get results then you are likely going to be disappointed. Your win is going to come in using email as a nurturing tool over a sales tool. Email should be there as a touch point element of the process at various stages of your communications process. I.e. when someone raises their hand to an initial date/conversation, let's say the format is a Zoom call, there would be various email confirmations, reminders and important information sent via email. These are important touch points that add to Guerilla Marketing's suggested subconscious touches in the trust building process.

2. **Outbound communication to lists:** Typically your outbound communications to lists are when initial communications have finished and your emails are no longer touch points linked to a meeting/event that has been scheduled. This could also be, for example, a voucher being sent or a document being delivered. The outbound communication is actually its own strategy and needs to follow the same principles that every overall strategy in this book should follow. Again, any strategy can technically have a 100% conversation rate if the offer is good enough, so when developing an email plan, keep this in mind.

Email marketing is great to determine who is engaging and who is inter-

1. keting communications via email. Take the bakery seen throughout this book, with the information they generated from their initial offer and conversation, they know about the person's family and what their favorite treats are. They could create a list in their CRM which has only those with families in it, leading to more personalized email marketing.

As you dive further into developing your strategy, nurturing, and sales cycles, you will see the common denominator is not how special our strategy is. If the number of hands you raise is great, but you have a low follow through, your call to action is too complicated or not quick enough but your offer is great and vice versa. Following this, the individual investment in the future relationship and great service are required to develop said relationship and make use of what Raise Your Hand Marketing has given to you.

Let's say you have a restaurant, and you have a list of 200 people who recently engaged with a 'free cocktail' raise your hand marketing offer online. In return for their offer, you received their email addresses and they answered a few questions about themselves, such as whether they have a family, their relationship status, what their favorite food is. The more you give them in terms of an offer, the more information you would get. At this point, they have received their cocktail voucher and the various conformations that come with it. What now? Well, first of all, there is an improvement opportunity here for immediate relationship gains. Many businesses who use this technique forget about the power of a planned appointment. They simply mail out the vouchers or have some automation that takes the human element out of it and hope for a little bit of guilt when the prospect uses the voucher. This does work but, nowhere near the power it could. For the restaurant in question, they could have stipulated that this is a cocktail experience and asked people to book a table in order to receive it. The prospects have to attend the restaurant in order to redeem their voucher anyway, so asking them to book an appointment gives the managers the time to plan and personalize the experience. Using the tools above, you could set up a Raise Your Hand fact finding email series that will help your team provide a better service. This Raise Your Hand email series could be 3-4 that start upon the confirmation of their booking and happen over the next week (You could set a rule that appointments need to be 1 week out in order for this to work). During this email chain, you can introduce elements of the restaurant, the team, and what is available to them ready for their arrival. As CRM's allow for single person action monitoring, you can see if people have clicked on certain items. You can use this to create questions & answers in emails, use this to build a picture of peoples' interests and more. If you saw that a person clicked on the breakfast menu on multiple occasions, that is a tell for them being interested in breakfast... rocket science! So when they arrive for booking, presenting the next 'date' which could be a breakfast offer may quite easily secure the next date with the prospects but also 'wow' them. 'How did they know?'

This isn't new. Data management and personalisation is done everywhere and every day. Large companies of the world are extremely good at doing this type of marketing on scale and their algorithms are constantly picking up on personalized notes about your data and offering products linked to that personalized note. You see this all of the time, with recommendations and thoughts of 'how did they figure that out'. Data companies are farming your data constantly, making it easier and easier for them to have you identify yourself, Raise Your Hand and deliver them further buying information. What you are trying to teach you here is that you are, in fact, a data company and the information you gather will enable you to deliver exceptional service and create the 'how did they know' statement which is so powerful to establish trust and long-term raving fans.

All in all, using Raise Your Hand Marketing in email is actually pretty simple. This should follow our target, offer, copy model and include calls to actions that simply ask for prospects to raise their hand for further value. This value could be digital; it could be something that you do not touch i.e., an automated document. This could also be physical i.e. a way to get people back into your physical location. As you are targeting a much wider audience in your marketing and aiming to generate much more self-identification from people at many different levels of want and need towards your product/service, there needs to be a staggered approach for different types of prospect. Some will be much closer to needing what you sell. They are generally physical conversations that will occur first and then enter a nurturing cycle which will include increasing levels of value heading towards the transaction.

Strategic Alliances

Raise Your Hand marketing can be used phenomenally to generate strategic alliance conversations or host beneficiaries. A host beneficiary is another business who has a similar target market to yours that will offer a hand raise opportunity to their customer base, usually in return for something. A strategic alliance is usually a business of the same target market for whom you may choose to undertake a mutually beneficial collaboration.

Just like with prospecting directly, you can use Raise Your Hand 'need' offers to get facetime with phenomenal strategic alliances that would usually be difficult to reach. You can use the various platforms of communication to do this but again, using ego to have a conversation first, can lead to the opportunity of positioning a relationship. Who you know and who you speak to has a direct reflection on the size of your business, this is a fact. Your network is your net worth. If you were to directly contact 10 potential partners about becoming a strategic alliance partner, due to their likely busyness, you may get somewhere with 1 or 2. If however you were to ask 10 businesses of similar industry/target market to join you in creating some collaborative content that will educate/solve a need for both of your target markets, and lean on their expertise, you will

This could work in any industry, not just business to business. If I was a restaurant and I wanted to link up with a local vineyard for example, I tailor my 'ask' around their expertise and offer them a great exposure opportunity. Due to ego, the vineyard would share any content you create and this would cement a relationship with permanent content. This would lead to a conversation where I could develop towards a strong collaboration.

The idea with Raise Your Hand marketing works in any relationship. You offer to provide a solution and use it to build on the relationship. Using strategic alliances as a distribution platform follows the same target, offer and copy rules. What's in it for the strategic alliance? What do they get out of it? They themselves need a compelling offer that solves a need in order to help you distribute to their network.

Number 1 rule! 'Get their email address'

There are typically 3 types of prospect that arrive from our Raise Your Hand marketing, these are:

- Yes, I would like the value proposition you are offering me (Conversation Opportunity)
- This sounds very interesting, but I would like more information (Conversation Opportunity)
- Engaged but not ready for a conversation (Email)

You need to get their email address as soon as possible. This is pretty easy on platforms like LinkedIn and if the enquiry came through the website, but other forms of social media like Instagram or Facebook are more difficult. Both of these platforms are very powerful for Raise Your Hand work, therefore you need to make sure that the are set up in the right way. If you are choosing to give a gift as your call to action, perhaps for a follow or an engagement on a post, you would recommend either talking to them on the platform to get this information, which is fast and powerful or sending them towards a landing page.

Choose the right tools (CRM, Data Capture)

People spend an awful lot of time deciding what the best CRM system is for them. A CRM system is there to help you make your conversations visual, keep data clean and maintain communications with your potential and existing customers. The bells and whistles can come later, but in reality, a CRM is for data capture and data management.

Choosing the right CRM system for data capture will depend on your preferred communications/visibility style as well as what system you are using to capture the data. There are about a million different tools and you could end up wasting time and money deciding which one is right. The major CRM systems like Hubspot, Salesforce, ActiveCampaign etc are a good place to start as these usually fit styles, offering automation for things like form fill completions such as automatic thank you emails.

A good CRM system for managing Raise Your Hand marketing campaigns should have the following:

- **Automated Emails** - Automation is a wonderful tool that is widely overcomplicated. Automation as a starting point can be used to create evergreen campaigns, which act as a constant build out of content that new prospects go to the beginning of when they join your database. By running some of the content asset strategies discussed in previous chapters, you can across 6 months build a few years worth of email marketing, full of highly engaging content. Imagine if every contact you got into your database then received emails for the next two years without you having to do anything? That would be awesome right? It is very simple to implement and you should start right away. Other forms of automation can be used to make sure you are communicating with people regularly and also internally, triggering follow up notifications and reminders to your team.

- **Pipeline/Funnel Management (Visual)** - A great feature of many CRMs. A visual board of the different stages of your conversation funnel with easy drag and drop features will be a great addition to your prospect management arsenal. This is a highly recommended addition and learning opportunity for you or your team.

- **Deal Information** - A good CRM will also allow you within your pipe-line to create notes on the different stages as that prospect passes through them. Having a place where you can keep information digitally is very important. That might sound very basic but you would be very surprised!

- **Tracking Tools** - Tracking tools within CRM systems are incredibly useful for Raise Your Hand marketing. As you will be communicating a lot with value and consistently sending information to people, the track-ing tools will allow you to set up scoring which will notify you when a person clicks or reacts to something, say 5 times. This is an indication of interest and allows you to make well thought out follow ups based on real time information. Once you have someone's data, you can also install better tracking on your website via your CRM which can also be used to score them based on page visits etc. Wouldn't that be interesting?

A tip for getting round **terrible** email builders would be to use Canva. Yes, Canva. The hardcore email specialists reading this may hate us for saying but by building image blocks in Canva, you can build a beautiful email marketing mailout easily with lots of clickable options for your readers.

When you choose your CRM, be it an industry specific one or general system, just make sure to take all the training and support you can from the company in order to become an expert yourself, typically this is free of charge as they want to retain you as a client.

16

Adapting Your Copy

You have now been introduced to various platforms. Not all platforms could be reviewed in these last chapters, otherwise this book would be thousands of pages long, but the point should have been made clear. The success of your marketing will still come down to the power of your offer and how you adapt your copy to said platform. If you pick any platform or distribution method that isn't showcased in the last chapter, try to understand the current usage and how it works with a marriage proposal driven marketing strategy, then make the switch and understand the impact of a well thought out Raise Your Hand campaign.

Adapting your copy to the platforms you choose is the only 'change' you need to worry about when it comes to the platform. Let's take a look at our Raise Your Hand Gardens Corp business and see which platforms they have initially chosen to test their offers. They are going to initially test 2 platforms per offer in their marketing plan which will give them good data and allow them to start tweaking and compounding their results:

Offer 1 - Las Vegas Gardens Of The Week

Platform for distribution 1 - Instagram Direct Messaging

The first platform RYH Gardens Corp will use is Instagram as a direct messaging tool. This is one of those tools where B2C direct messaging is still a use-able, to an extent, platform when done on a small and precise scale. It also allows for RYH Gardens corp to engage with the prospect outside of the message by looking at their profiles, liking photos, etc.

Their goal is to generate at least one opportunity per week and therefore they have set an initial target of asking 20 homeowners per week using Instagram to be involved in the series. Alongside this, they are going to start actively engaging with the homeowners profiles to build more familiarity for the prospect with the brand.

Using Instagram, they will utilize hashtags such as #mygarden #lasvegasgardens #gardensoflasvegas #livinginlasvegas and more to find profiles that actively share their homes. These home accounts are rife on Instagram due to it being a highly ego-driven platform and that everyone wants to be an influencer.

The initial message to be sent will be the following;

'Hi X, I hope you don't mind us sending you a message but we absolutely love what you have done with your home. We are actually looking for homeowners to be a part of our new 'Las Vegas Gardens of the Week' series and having taken a look at your profile, I think you would be an amazing addition. All we would need to do is send our team round to take a few snaps and then a piece would be shared to our social media and database. I can see that you are actively trying to build an audience for your home so I am sure this would help you reach more people! We can chat here if you would like to reply or just send your phone number and I will give you a call'

Dissecting that message, you can see the offer was presented in a calm way and it immediately brought ego into play. It supported the goals of the prospect and showcased that we think they have an amazing home. This is going to do nothing but bring them joy and the response rate for this message would be great. The call to action offers two forms of communication that are simple, but equally, these will need to be tested. If RYH Gardens Corp at the same time actively follows, likes posts, and comments on the profile, even shares the accounts photos to their page, this will help build the conversion rate and trust from this campaign.

Platform for distribution 2 - Strategic Alliance

Utilizing Strategic Alliances for this offer will create two assets. Firstly, it will be a great initiation of future relationships with businesses that have the same target as you, and secondly, it will be a low-cost way to generate high conversion rates for your offer. You are leveraging your strategic alliances pre-built trust with the prospect, this will be a great foundation for you to build upon.

Presenting your offer to the strategic alliance needs to be done in a way that again brings in the psychology you have learned throughout this book. You can reach out via socials, email or the phone as examples to do this. Let's use email as an example:

Hi X,

How are you? It was great to see you last month at X event.

I am just wondering if you might be able to help us with a project that we believe will aid both of our businesses. We are launching a new series online called 'Las Vegas Gardens Of The Week' to promote fantastic homes and gardens across Las Vegas. This will be a great opportunity for the homeowner to showcase their hard work. Our goal is to use this to create educational content for our audience but also to showcase ideas for people in a highly visual way. As your customer base are all homeowners, are there people we could potentially reach out to together to ask them if they would like to be involved?

We will be paying for the production and in return for your help, we would love to include a segment in the posts about you and what you can provide the community. Our expectation due to the size of the homeowner market and fact that the home is a highly followed phenomenon on social media, this will generate some fantastic traffic and view counts.

Should we discuss it on the phone so I can explain this a little better? Just let me know and I will call you tomorrow.

Many thanks,

Y'

This copy has a few things in it worth discussing. Firstly, it showcases the power of what RYH Gardens Corp wants to do and the potential audience size, kicking up exposure thoughts for the potential strategic alliance. The offer to them for exposure in return will peak their interest and alongside this, you are using ego in the copy to drive thoughts that they have an exceptional customer base. The call to action is simple; instead of this heading into a back and forth email chain or simply offering the chance for them to say no, it focuses on the conversation. Even with no response, RYH Gardens corp could follow up with a call or text, even dropping into the strategic alliances offices and it wouldn't feel out of the blue to bring up the offer.

The above is an example of how the offer can be presented with these platforms.

There will be many other ways RYH Gardens Corp could do this as well.

Offer 2 - Free Grass Food!

This is a simple offer and is a great example of a giveaway. The platforms used for the example are the following:

Platform one - social media advertising

Social media platforms are going to give you the greatest reach for the lowest cost therefore they are the perfect testing ground for your ads. The suggestion with these types of ads, by professionals, is to have lots of different tests trying different copy, video, and imagery. If you want to do this, there is no stopping you but for those reading this book that want to get visibility of their markets appetite for their offer, try the following to start with on your A/B testing journey:

2 different images - Pick two different image types that you will use for your test. RYH Gardens Corp has decided to choose an image of the feed itself and an image of a beautiful home they recently worked on and have permission to use. This looks to test two different ideas; the first being whether or not it is the product the prospect is going to be most interested in or whether they will best respond to aspiration techniques.

2 different videos - To create comparisons between both explanations of the gift and aspirational content these videos will contrast each other in order to test engagement. The first video will be an explainer filmed by RYH Gardens Corp asking whether people would like the gift, showcasing the gift in the video. The second will be an aspirational video that was shot of their previous work. Both of these will be different in terms of their target so this will allow RYH Gardens to test the results and see which one creates better conversation.

Once they have the ad content, they are going to write two small versions of the copy which can be A/B tested, following the rules discussed in prior chapters. RYH Gardens Corp may need to test various versions of the copy. A good rule of thumb would be about 10% of people you ask say yes, this means in theory from an ad perspective 10% of the clicks to your site. Other measurables will be followed through to completing the offer, engagement levels in the conversation and of course, the number of people progressing through the sales cycle.

Copy one would read something like this:

Do you have a garden in Las Vegas?! We are giving away 1 LB of premium grass feed worth over $40 to 50 lucky homeowners in Las Vegas! No catch, just send us a DM saying 'Me please!' And one of our team will be in touch! Whilst stocks last'

The second copy would perhaps try an alternative call to action like:

Calling all gardening lovers in Las Vegas! We would like you to try our premium grass feed, completely free. There's only 50 1LB bags available so if you want one, be quick and just comment 'me please!' On this post. If you have a friend you want to love you too, tag them and let them know about the offer!'

These copies do a few things. They lean on a product we know everyone with a garden will be interested in. It also brings only in and asks them to make a simple call to action. There is nothing in this ad that is salesly or marriage proposal oriented, at all!

These ads could well be stronger. For the sake of this book, they are a simple example and whilst you can use them for ideas, you will want to test out different words and ideas until you are happy with the uptake. Chances are for little investment, however, RYH Gardens Corp will have 50 small conversations with homeowners in the target market who will form trust with the brand. They will also have the opportunity, when they ask further questions, to develop the relationship further.

Post this conversation, RYH Gardens Corp can then begin to tailor other marketing efforts to their new relationship needs and build the relationship further. They're on the way to their goal, and who says they need to stop at 50?

Platform two - email marketing

Email marketing can be used to communicate with the current database that RYH Gardens Corp has and distribute the offer. A/B testing should also be used here before sending out an email to the whole database. The way this should be done to not burn your whole database with an offer is to send out your offer initially to 10%, breaking that into two 5% sized chunks.

Copy for the email should be like the following & you can tweak different elements. This is just one example, but it should help you visualize the outcome you want and see where the rules are used.

'Hi X,

We hope you are having a great 2023 so far! We can't believe the spring season is arriving in a few months and to celebrate, we would like to offer you a free 1 LB of grass feed from our friends over at Y company. The grass feed is valued at over $40 and we only have 50 LBs available. I am sure this would be useful for you and we would love to know how your grass loves the food!

I have attached a few images of the product below as well as some before and after photos.

If you would like to claim your free 1LB of food, simply respond back with your address and phone number and I will have this posted out.

Any questions let me know!

Y'

This is a super simple email. You don't want to over do it, less is more with these types of communication. This is an example of a direct email, not a newsletter style email but it follows the rules and will be successful.

Conclusion:

There has been an awful lot of practical insight into your target market, offers, copy and the distribution to suspects with a view of turning them into prospects. Whilst this book cannot give you tailored examples to your industry personally, it should provide an idea flow you need to develop your own overall strategies that will deliver the conversations you need.

To close off the theory and the initial conversation parts of this book, let's revisit the whole market concept once more to make sure you are ready for the next steps.

It can be very easy to slip into old habits and mindsets. Especially during the first month or two of building your farm. Due to the different types of workload, managing relationships can feel like more than you're used to. If you think you are a person that is going to be unproductive or miss things if the workload gets too high, just start smaller. You are reading this book because you want to grow your business and have better relationships, you already want to do the work.

Now that you understand raising hands is the stepping stone to more conversations, you will be able to clearly see whether your offer is working, whether the call to action is efficient or not and whether your target market is delivering the right type of conversation.

What happens when something doesn't work?

You are going to face things not working, so it is important that you are clear on why. Your knowledge of Raise Your Hand Marketing strategies will give you tweakable areas and allow you to make sure that you aren't fixing what isn't broken. Typically things not working with Raise Your Hand Marketing can be put into three buckets. This may sound very simple but it will allow you to categorize what isn't working, making it easier to adapt and improve:

1. **Low number of offer acceptances** - This is very simply, your offer isn't getting enough value across or the copy isn't correct to present that value.

2. **High offer acceptances but low follow through to conversation** - Your offer is strong, but your call to action or acceptance process is not the correct form of communication or breaks the 'one thing' rule described in the call to action chapter. Simple is better.

3. **Low relationship building** - This is usually down to your target market or the questions you are asking.

If RYH Gardens Corp had this problem, let's say with their free grass food giveaway, and their ad generated 100 interested parties for the offer but only 20 people actually provided the information necessary to warrant the giveaway. In this situation, RYH Gardens would need to analyze what is being asked of people and how much they are expecting the prospect to do to get their offer. The offer itself is dropping off around 80% which is too high, so simpler measures can be put in place to make sure things improve. It is often a thought process that the conversation needs to happen immediately but the prospect does not yet have anything in their hand. If you are facing this problem, then the action would be to try different forms of call to action, simpler forms, and perhaps make the delivery process more conversational. There is nothing stopping RYH Gardens Corp from delivering these by hand to initiate conversation or following up to see how the prospect is doing with some instruction based communications (further value). Typically, tweaks to the call to action will improve this. The simpler it is, the more offer completions you will get. You do, however, need to make sure you are getting what you need to further the conversation, so if this becomes so simple you are not, then the offer needs to be revisited so it creates more urgency and more value for the prospect. Remember, the higher the perceived value the more information you will receive and the stronger the conversation will be.

Another example of this would be if we have a hair salon that was giving away free blow drys. They couldn't get the volume of people to say yes, but when they conducted the free blow drys, their conversion to a scheduled appointment was 75%. In this scenario, we need to look at the target, offer, and copy. The target could be too wide, therefore our platform may not be getting enough of the right people to see it. A good exercise would be to look at who did accept and focus efforts on that age range, for example. The hair salon could also re-write their copy to make sure that the offer is clearer or test and measure different types of imagery or video that creates that emotional and aspirational value for the prospect. Following this, they know that once people are sat in the chair, they have a high value, so more effort can be put into the communication process, more value added to the offer or even simpler calls to actions brought into play. In this scenario, the salon just needs the booking and their conversation will come at the appointment.

It's not that your strategy won't work, it's that your target, your offer, your copy or your call to action is letting you down.

A common learning mistake

The biggest mistake you can make, however, is to jump in too hard with excitement. It's common for people to read books, get new ideas, and go all in for a few weeks until the work arrives and then become inconsistent. When you are building a farm that will provide for you for years to come, it is going to include a lot of work, sacrifice and patience. This book has discussed the absolute requirement for consistency and pure focus on the prospects' needs many times. Without those to two things becoming habit,

You have heard theory of habit building and that it takes on average 21 days of consistency for a habit to be formed. Warren Buffett once said the chains of habit are too light to be felt until they are too heavy to be broken.

If you are going to try to implement the ideas described in this book, make sure that you commit to the theory and commit to conversation for at least 90 days. This is a full quarter of the year and will allow you to properly measure the results. There will be work, there will be thinking, there will be relationships, sales, and a few frustrating times in those 90 days, but it will go by in a blink.

I promise you, if you commit to making the change from hunter to farmer and fully push yourself to becoming the number one business in your industry at caring and providing for customers and prospects needs, the results will explain themselves.

The final part of this book discusses the first date, questions, and understanding buyer psychology.

PART 3

17

After Raising a Hand

Time to dive into what happens when you have raised a hand. You will see some examples of what to do, and what not to do, using our volunteer business RYH Gardens Corp. Most of you have a lot of experience selling your product or service, dealing with customers and developing relationships. That being said, the type of prospect you have to deal with here is different and it requires you to have made that switch from hunter to farmer. Due to this person being behind in their trust for you when compared to someone who has sought you out specifically for your service or a referral, for example, they can seem like hard work and, like the compound effect says, it can feel like they are going nowhere until out of the blue, an opportunity arrives. Planting front-of-mind seeds and building trust, as well as consistent information gathering to tailor opportunities that you feel meet the prospects needs, will help you in the long run. The way that you gather this information and nurture prospects towards buying is very simple questions and consistent follow up.

Your hand raising doesn't stop with the initial marketing strategy. It's vital to continue your value creation, finding need through questions and solving problems until the need matches your product or service.

Once you have successfully raised a hand and created an initial engagement point, you have prospects and the next step in the ladder of loyalty is shopper, where a lead is officially generated. In order for someone to become a shopper, they must be taking action beyond your original offer in relation to your product or service. If they do not do this straight away, the prospect simply needs further nurturing and further value from you until their needs match one of your products or services.

Moving KPIS from Sales To Number Of Conversations

You were asked to change your view on what success looks like in marketing. If you can find a strategy that successfully raises the hands of prospects at a rate that is 3-4 times larger than a traditional sales approach strategy, you have a very successful foundation.

With conversations as the KPI (key performance indicator, which is a measurement you use vs the output to determine your level of success), you increase the chances of you reaching your target number because conversations are relatively controllable and leads are much less so. Think back to the business chassis in the five ways, where instead of getting caught up in the outcome, you focus on what you can control and you compound through to create massive results. If you are reporting our conversations and having your KPIs based around those conversations, and each team member in charge of increasing the success of each stage of conversation is clear on what they are doing. Plus, from the business chassis, you know that a simple 10% increase of five stages will not lead to a 10% increase in the results, it will lead to a 60+ percent increase in the results.

Setting up your team for success:

Another common occurrence is that KPIs for the team members are based on results that the team members control. A common one is for marketing people giving them a sales based KPI that will trigger some sort of commission. Many owners wonder why their marketing staff never seem to push beyond what is expected and rarely report a week where their time has been over 50% utilized effectively.

Setting KPIs to the number of conversations for manual platforms, touch points for leveraged ones, touch points/follow ups is an easy, controllable way to manage KPIs. Yes, they aren't sold yet but that isn't marketing's job. Their job is to raise hands from suspect to prospect and make sure that prospect gets the offer they have been promised and the target is right so that the percentage of prospects becoming a lead and eventually a customer is increasing.

The result is that your team member is directly involved in and controls their KPI. What does this mean? Well, if you have a marketing person who is an appointment setter for the secondary conversation, lets say their job is to call suspects and ask them to raise their hand to some sort of value (your offer), should this person have KPIs & Commission based on the number of meetings they book in or the number of sales the sales person eventually makes? It seems very, very simple. It is obviously the element they can control, as the sales person could let them down and create friction within the team.

18

Your First Date - Questions & Buying Siganls

The first date is very simply the first conversation, either digital or physical, that you have with a new prospect. It can be easy to take the new high volume of conversations you will be having and screw them up with excitement that you are about to sell a lot. These prospects have however very simply just accepted some value you have created for them. They do not trust you yet and you don't know much about them, therefore, you must use this initial communication wisely. You have been taught to build know, like, and trust, as well as gather information. Now is the time to put a plan and map in place based on the offers you developed in part one.

Returning to the Ladder of Loyalty

Raving Fan

Advocate

Member

Customer

Shopper

Prospect

Suspect

As you embark on your initial conversation, you should be already geared up with tools and pre-set questions that will help in finding information that will identify current challenges/needs. If you do this correctly, inviting the prospect to the next stage of your nurturing process should be straightforward and carry a high conversion rate, as you will again be able to identify something they will raise their hand too. You should prepare these for each eventuality from your questions and be armed with your further hand raises for certain challenges that come up. These could link to you, which turns the prospect into a lead, or they could be linked to the industry where you can provide support, expertise, or strategic alliance referrals. If you are being rejected for further communications after your first conversation, you have not identified the correct need or have proposed marriage. Each prospect may be slightly different than the other but as long as they are in the correct target market, you should be able to provide value. Sales is not and should not be viewed as a one-size-fits-all process. Every conversation you have with a prospect will be slightly different and it is your job to nurture what is important to them, raising their hand further and further down the line until such trust is built so that they wouldn't look anywhere else but you.

As you begin to think about questions and mapping out the different scenarios that come up, look at your current sales cycle to think about the stages that will occur during it and currently when a lead is generated. Typically during our first conversation, there will be a number of the conversations that give buying signals (a need that matches your product/service), therefore these should move into the lead management element of your CRM/spreadsheet and into your normal sales cycle. If the offer acceptance is very simply an acceptance and the prospect doesn't showcase immediate problems you can solve with your product or service, this will lead to a different set of questions that will be geared towards finding information.

Using Questions to develop conversation

A whole sales pitch should be centered around a set of questions that leads your prospect to the desired outcome/need being showcased, so that you build the relationship and offer support, in the way that suits them and their personality type. You should be able to map out exactly how you want the conversation to go via questions. The question should be written in a way that gives you information to test buying signals/need, as well as give you the information that you need to create a tailored offer for further relationship development.

There are typically 3-4 types of ways you can ask your questions and you should always include a question/answer process as the reciprocation they prospect owes you for the value you are providing. The higher the value of your offer, the more information you can ask for and likewise, the higher the value of the offer, the more likely you are going to be able to have a human conversation with that prospect, which is the communication method that will bring trust the fastest. Not all offers you run will lead to physical, and likely you would not have the time to service all of these anyhow but that is the end goal. Even with your lower value offers, the forms you use, for example, will give you the power to identify the needs of a prospect and begin to see their potential value should they become a customer. Due to their self-identification and progress through the ladder of loyalty, the relationship with them becomes more valuable and therefore you can invest further into the relationship with less risk and more precision due to your knowledge of their needs and answers to their questions.

To begin thinking about questions, you very simply need to explore what information would allow you to build a profile on someone and understand their needs in relation to your product, service or industry. What problems are they facing that could be solved by something you have expertise in? This is the same exercise as the wide market need finding you did earlier on, just more focused as the person you are asking the question to is now a target market prospect, someone you want to have a business relationship with.

If you were an accountant, for example, and you were having a conversation with someone in the construction industry for an ebook, you may ask a question like 'What is the current attitude of the banks in your industry for loans/raising capital?' which could lead into 'Are you growing organically or is the business capital intensive?'. These questions are great and the outcome for our accountant is that we now know if someone is having a challenge with the banks, whether they take on outside capital and debt as well as their general view on growth. These answers would lead the accountant to discussing their set up for raising capital, how they handle tax with equity raises and more, all leading to either a 'Would it be a terrible idea to have a 20 minute chat on that? We have dealt with a number of clients who have faced the same scenario and it would probably be beneficial so you can save time?" if they expressed highly positive interest or some sort of further value that solves the problem if they were more reserved. If the answer was not something their product or service could directly solve, they could say, 'I have a client who has worked in the industry for a long time, he has grown a number of businesses and I am sure would be happy to share some thoughts with you. Would that be helpful? I can make an introduction'. Having your alliances, hand raises, and key people that will help you provide value is important. Clients you have strong relationships with that will help you by chatting and providing expertise will nearly always end up in them shouting great things about you.

I have even seen businesses paying their clients to do this for 30 minutes of their

time. This is an ego stroke for them and nearly every time they raise their hand to get involved. Can you start to see how conversations drive value?
By keeping your questions linking back to need and generally about them, you can quite quickly see opportunities that further value can be provided.

The aim is always to make them feel like they are making the decision, so when you do finally get to hand raise, ask their permission and allow them to feel in control. You have identified a need, now allow them to see the solution and raise their hand.

Questions should be used at ALL stages and for ALL company types in developing relationships and data. Even if the likelihood is that someone will take up your offer and buy, there should be a set of questions you ask. These questions should be asked in return for their offer or as part of a transaction process.

Nearly all relationships in any business will eventually lead to a 'Can I have some more info on what you do?' or 'How can you help me' sort of question. Sales gurus teach that you should ask questions until the prospect asks one; this is where your job has been successful. This is more so for those businesses who are non-consumer but this will also happen in those industries, especially if you are using Raise Your Hand marketing. With questions, it's very easy to flow into a conversation that doesn't seem aggressive and it is simple to see where needs and problems arise.

How would RYH Gardens Corp set up their questions and handle the conversation element to Raise Your Hand Marketing? Let's use the grass feed offer as an example for furthering conversation and presenting the next stages of the relationship.

RYH Gardens Corp picked owners of detached properties in Las Vegas as their target market for this offer due to the fact that most of these homeowners would have gardens. The offer was chosen as a wide market need, the fact that everyone with a garden would be interested in a free gift that would help them create the garden of their dreams. This brings in aspiration and emotion, as it provides a solution to the owner that they will have a nice garden. The offer would cut through the noise of those with no interest in maintaining and improving their gardens, as no one uninterested would be raising their hand for some feed they would have to administer themselves. The anticipated result, due to the exclusive number of gifts RYH Gardens were giving away at just 50, with a target market much greater is that they can ask more questions due to this exclusivity and people are aware that they need to be quick to accept the offer. This urgency will allow RYH to ask for more information as it enhances perceived value.

The two routes that RYH Gardens decided upon for the call to action and the accepting of the offer was a direct digital conversation on their social media & email platforms, as well as a form for those on their website seeing the offer. These two call to actions have slightly different question approaches therefore both are broken down below:

Form

A form is very simply a set of questions that people fill out in order to submit their interest in whatever it is you are offering. You can customize the forms questions, making some required answers, in order for you to receive the information you need to fulfill their expectations as well as information you want to gather in order to develop the relationship further. When someone hits a landing page, they are clicking on a direct offer and want what it is you present. If this is the case, why is there so much drop off from traffic to completion? If you remember the copy chapter of this book, it's often due to the form being too complicated or when their expectations are not met, leaving them feeling like they do not trust the offer. Deciding on what questions to ask is going to be based on the value of your offer. In this case, the value is about $40 but the added exclusivity means we can ask for a bit more:

Q1 - What is your name?
Q2 - What is your email address?
Q3 - What is your phone number?

Q4 - What is your mailing address?

Q5 - How big is your garden roughly? (sq ft)

Q6 - Do you maintain your garden yourself or via a professional?

Q7 - What is your favorite flower?

The above starts to paint a picture of who your prospect is via a few questions associated with their garden as well as the key information we need to actually know who they are and further market to them. This is quite a few questions but RYH Gardens Corp believe its a fair reciprocation for the gift. If they see high traffic to the form, but low conversion, they can tweak the form. If they see high traffic and high conversion, remembering they only have an exclusive number of gifts to give-away in this initial campaign, they could tweak the form to be more intuitive and

As a follow up to the grass feed gift, RYH Gardens could begin to send tailored specific content about certain garden types, experience on certain types of the city and further gifts of flowers based on their favorite. Once these conversations have been developed and the relationship is blossoming, a phone call or offer to come and see their garden for a free consultation would be the best start to drive a sale. It is also likely that with the tailored content and their being lots of capture opportunities all over RYH Gardens corps marketing and website, that there will be an increased number of people that will ask for quotes there and then.

Conversation

In this case RYH Gardens Corp's conversion is going to be digital. Their ad has a call to action with 'DM' or 'comment below'. Your scripting for how to deal with this is just the same as the form, you just get to have an actual one to one conversation with them to get it. The conversation could be like the following:

RYH: 'Thanks so much for registering interest in our free gift, I just need to ask some questions so I can make sure it's the right feed, and of course, where you are. Is that all ok with you?' With this, you are seeking permission and keeping control seemingly with the prospect. Most will say yes, of course, some will drop out, however this is a good thing as it continues to refine who is going to be worth developing a relationship with. Following this the person manning the platform will ask a few questions that they need and also some interesting information on the prospect. This could be 'How long have you lived in the area?', 'Do you love DIY gardening?' or 'We are seeing a lot of renovations at the moment, any plans on the horizon?'. These questions build a profile and they will be useful in the future, or even in that moment if the prospect discusses ideas with you. If they said yes to plans or gave you some insight they need help, you could offer them a call to discuss this and therefore complete the lead generation process.

What you are seeing here in this chapter is why we use questions. Revert back to the bakery again from the initial chapters in this book. They used an offer to generate engagement and then used questions to further their relationship along and eventually wow the customer, creating a lifetime purchase opportunity.

A key point to remember is that your questions in the initial conversation should not include any marriage proposals...

You are a data company, too.

Elon Musk is famous for saying that Tesla is not a car manufacturer, Tesla is a data company. Every mile that gets driven sends data back to the company, that means they are creating data on roads, cities, driver demographics/styles all over the world. What they choose to do with that in the end is not yet known, but have you noticed something? Elon and the team always seem to come up with stuff that people want and buy in a cult-like manner. Some of this will be due to the brand he is building for himself, but actually it's probably because they listen and they focus on memorable experiences that people actually want in that moment.

Where some may feel like personalisation and experience driven additions to your service or freebies giveaways etc are a waste of time, they become memorable and are huge assets due to the data you get from the customer as they have this experience. This data enables us to market more easily, customize experience and target what truly matters to that customer, enabling you to build easier relationships and better businesses. I fully believe that you are all data companies and you should be seeking to generate as much knowledge out of our customer base as possible all of the time. This will not only help us improve service but it will help us make a lot more in terms of profit too.

My question to you at this stage would be, what data would help you build a better business? This is the data that should form part of your questions and part of your Raise Your Hand strategy. If you know that learning, your customers' address or perhaps the number of kids they have, or where they went to school will help you build a better understanding of them as well as a better service, then these are the things you will receive in return for the value you am giving to the customer. What would you need to know about your prospects to enhance their experience with you? This is the starting point in developing your questions.

Raise Your Hand marketing is as much about the sales pipeline as it is about the data. Every time you speak to someone, you are collecting data. This is very important to know and by going into life as a business person or marketer with this in your brain, you will think differently, a few steps ahead and always be on plan.

Humanize The Relationship, automate everything else

Automation is great, however, humanizing your relationship is single handedly the most important thing when it comes to initially building your pipeline. Do not run before you can walk. People constantly decide that they do not want to put time and effort physically into their sales pipeline and that it should all be automated. That may be the case in the future, but if you want speed and growth quickly, engaging either in human conversation or via messenger platforms will speed up your process. Someone filling out a form is a perfect opportunity to enter into human engagement, someone clicking through your 'hand raise' call to action on an email is the perfect opportunity to engage. There are so many great opportunities lurking in plain sight for you to increase your engagement, build relationships, and strengthen your business. It takes effort but it will lead to you being able to use the word only in a short period of time.

There are phenomenal automation tools out there and you believe that anything outside of the direct engagement opportunities should be automated. Various platforms like Hubspot, ActiveCampaign, Salesforce, etc, are fantastic and simple tools that will help you automate your communication with potential customers, existing customers and past customers.

What is the goal of automation, especially in email? This is where many people go wrong, the goal with email and automation should be to see how people are interacting with your content and use that to engage physically. I.e. if someone who has raised their hand to previous value offerings opens an email automation I have sent 3 times in a row, clicking on the other hand raises opportunities I have laid out in the email, is that person worth checking in on? Yes, of course.

19

Lifetime Customers

When you started reading this book, you were asked to make a decision to change your mindset from short term single transaction focused marketing to relationship marketing that develops lifetime customers. All of the things you have learnt in this book will take care of the major bottleneck for most businesses, the initial conversation with their target market. If that bit has become easy, then there should be an influx of business, right? Perhaps. The thing with it being simply the initial part of the relationship is that there is still a lot of work to do. You know this now. There are a few ways that you can ensure moving into the relationship building cycle with your new prospects will be a success:

- Tailored Communication

You make all communication, digital or physical, tailored to that person you are talking to and you are totally abundant. This asset will bring trust quickly and all of those problems you find yourself talking about are things you can help with to create further trust.

- Exceptional delivery

Second to none, exceptional delivery and knowing your numbers is a vital key to retaining and adding new lifetime customers. Understanding your capacity levels at initial offer, proposal levels, and eventually the sale, isn't a negotiation. Remember the beer analogy, when you order a pint of beer but get half pint back? Make sure you are delivering full pints and a little added value on top

- Trust - Developing raving fans

Raving fans arrive when customers feel that you are their brand. They trust you enough that they cannot wait to shout about you. This is why trust early on and exceptional service, as well as added value is very very important to buying lifetime customers. Make sure also your referral strategy is strong and the offer is big enough that potential referees raise their hand (yep, just a normal raise your hand strategy that follows the exact same target, offer, copy rules with a distribution platform)

- Membership

Another key thing to ensure lifetime relationships are maximized is introducing membership. This could come in the form of subscriptions or it could come in the form of loyalty clubs. As well as this, membership could be seen as a sign up and pay monthly or a rewards building scheme with you. You can have varying types of membership and whilst a book needs to be and will be written on membership, the point should be clear. How can you lock in repeat business? Offer discounts to members? First access to new products for members? Exclusive events? These offers to entice membership still follow the same rules. Big offer and the utilization of ego, exposure, emotion, or aspiration.

Marketing to new, existing and past customers, as well as potential alliances is all the same. Your initial hand raising tactics can be used over and over with these groups and they should just follow the simple rules to raise hands.

Buying:

There could be a whole other book written on sales and there is no way to go through this process in depth in a few paragraphs, but the focus at this point shouldn't be there. You are an expert, and you know your business, and there is no blueprint for when you should present the offer of what it is you do and how you can help or when this is the right time. The best way to do this in very simple terms is to have a written sales process where key metrics can be recorded such as the initial conversation about your services, the proposal/pricing, the follow up and the contractual/purchase process. You can measure the conversations into these key areas and you will see where the diminishing effects kick in as the funnel gets tighter, providing you with a great way to make measurable tweaks to your process. As you will be having far more conversations and engaging with far more of your target audience, this measurement process is even easier as it does get simpler and more effective with higher volume.

The simple rule is when the prospects' needs match something you offer as part of your product or service suite and you have the ability to solve their problem, you have to present a conversation where this can be discussed. If you are presenting this and they do not accept, the need is not strong enough and you need to go back to developing further offers where you can gather more information, build more know, like, and trust and remain front of mind for when they do have a problem you can solve with a transactional relationship. If you are feeling like you aren't getting enough 'leads' from your strategies, then go back and understand whether your target market is correct, the offer is strong enough to get that correct target market through, the offer is strong enough for you to find the correct need and the copy/call to action is driving the volume necessary for you to be understand this.

It all comes down to those three or four key areas. Whether it's your marketing strategy not yielding volume hands being raised, your actual conversations being low or your leads, they all trace back to the value you are creating and how wide the problem you are solving is.

Crisis Management

You are going to screw up at some point. You have all had a bad experience with a business before and when they attempted to market to you again, you said something on the lines of ' as if'. This is due to the company not having a problem management process and making sure that every crisis is turned into an opportunity. A crisis offers a redemption opportunity which can actually strengthen your relationship beyond its original state. NEVER EVER make this about you. Spending money to re-do, offering time for free or large value that carries a cost is the best investment you can make. If you were in the wrong, make it right no matter what. Suck up the cost and buy your lifetime customer. The mistake is not theirs, so they should receive royal treatment to make sure their view of you is back on track. This is worth whatever it costs and again, please, do not waste this perfect lifetime customer opportunity by being arrogant or not wanting to outlay to fix what you caused.

Zappos, the shoe company, delivered the wrong shoes to me once. They could have asked me to return them which is what most companies would have done and maybe that would have been fine. Instead, they chose to wow me by sending someone out, from the company, to replace them first hand. This wasn't necessary but it won me over. There are so many examples of bad service or communication being screwed up due to ego. These are amazing, wonderful opportunities for you to win and buy a lifetime customer.

19

The Initial Goals

The initial goals of this book were the following:

1. How to have structured conversations with more people than you have ever spoken to before

The strategies laid out in this book and the theories you have been walked through will allow you to reach this goal in a controlled way. You may not believe it right now, but when you get going, I know you will have a smile on your face. Brad and I look forward to hearing about just how many conversations you actually have and how your business is growing. The structural elements of this goal was all really about making sure you have a plan and that you are not trying to get married on the first date.

So put your engagement rings away and buy your prospects a drink. Show your full potential, be chivalrous in your communication and focus very simply on the next step and what that person needs out of the relationship. Each one of your strategies will give you a different set of steps, so start small, start simple, and be consistent. Be overprepared, think about scenarios in advance, and be ready. As well as this, what did we say was one of the most important traits of a very successful marketing plan? Consistency. You cannot compound success without consistency. When you find something that works for you, go for it and make sure to continue experimenting with larger scale strategies, increasing small bits at a time and making sure that you retain quality as you move towards the overall goal of your campaign, which in most cases is a revenue number. Starting with the end goal in mind will help you plan backwards to now, allowing for an effective plan to be put in place and the exact number of conversations you need to achieve your goals.

2. How to build a strong marketing machine so that you control and limit the number of new customers you bring into your business

You have learned that conversations are the lifeblood of any business and conversations are actually a near 'controllable' outcome you can rely on with wide market solutions to challenges commonly being faced. By using the theory laid out in this book, you will be able to deliver offers and copy across any platform you choose as well as measure it so that your further action and secondary hand raises are effective. Doing this, and knowing where a 'lead' is generated, will allow you to connect your marketing plan into your sales process in a smooth and measurable way. This will enable you to pick the number of conversations you have as you will have visibility on what is working so increase/decrease based on your ability to deliver. Should your sales system work the way you have planned it to and you have worked in the relevant margins of safety, you will be able to predict your growth and limit the number of customers you take on, creating exclusivity and making sure that your delivery performance is upheld.

You will begin to find that different platforms deliver prospects at different points of their journey. In the ladder of loyalty, there are steps between prospect and shopper and steps between shopper and customer. These will be different for all of you but they need figuring out. Tweak, change, test, and enjoy the process. As a society, we are trained to think that everyone is the same, when in fact every single person who raises their hand to your business is different. It is your job to match their needs with something you can provide, either as a freemium offer/value builder or via one of your products/services. Lifetime customers begin their transactional journey with you the moment their need matches up with your product or service. This moment, with the trust that has been built into it through conversation, creates harmony of mindset, no buyer's remorse and the perfect foundation for a future relationship. It's your job to farm these moments via conversation and great service. Becoming a customer of yours has to be exclusive, and if their needs do not match then they are not ready and it would be a disservice to sell to them.

3. How to profitably buy lifetime customers

Throughout this book the word profitability has been discussed frequently. The obvious reason why is that without profitability there is little point being in business. You are here to build a commercial, profitable enterprise that could work without you should you choose to. This book has shown you what a lifetime customer is and what it takes to buy them. Raise Your Hand marketing should allow you to create the best return on investment you have ever experienced from the various platforms available to you.

Compound your plan

This book has touched briefly on the point that the compound effect is often seen as the 8th wonder of the world as per Albert Einstein's age old statement. This was best taught with the simple question, would you rather have a penny that doubles every day for 30 days or $3M right now. A lot of the kids in the room said $3M, obviously, which would give them an amazing life right now and they would be off to the races! Those who said a penny, would have $10M by the time 30 days ran up, yet would have to wait until the last few days to overtake their peers. Compounding works like an exponential curve, and Warren Buffett says the chains of habit are too light to be felt until they are too strong to be broken. You are a creature of habit and having a strong yet simple plan with daily conversation driving tasks will keep you at ease and moving forward towards your goals.

In reality, marketing is pretty simple. Marketing is about communicating with your target market and in the right way which creates value for them and educates them on your business.

The compound effect works with marginal gains. It works by making yourself 1% better each day and not being fearful of expanding what is working. Raise Your Hand marketing should give you strategies that work consistently and predictably, therefore reducing your fear dramatically. Fear, as I'm sure you have heard before, stands for 'false evidence appearing real', and fear is the one thing that truly holds you back as entrepreneurs and business people. You haven't built a business before that's larger than the one you're currently running, in most cases. This means that in reality, growth is an unknown space for you. Fear is what will hold you back and will stop you achieving the goals you set out early in this book. By backtracking from your goals and building a plan that delivers the exact number of conversations you need to have in order to achieve your goals, there is nothing stopping you other than other fears and diminishing quality with size.

Lean into the growth, allow yourself to be uncomfortable, and write down what's making you uncomfortable. Is it the extra spend? Is it the bigger team? Is it a sense of perhaps you not belonging? These are all questions that go through business owners' heads and managers all the time, plus many more. I once heard the phrase 'a problem written down is a problem solved', so as a last exercise in this book. write down what problems you think your mindset will face and if you're facing any at the moment. This will help you immensely in solving the challenge or issue you are facing at that time.

As you've worked through this book and all of the exercises given to you, I would hope that you are excited to implement and get moving today. Due to the simplicity and a very required component of consistency, there is no better time to start than right now. So, as you are gearing up to launch your plan, where can you implement Raise Your Hand marketing right now? Are there conversations you've had in the last week where you can revisit them and offer some sort of value that person could need right now? Are there leads that you thought were dead that most likely have a problem that needs solving you can help with?

Closing Question

You have come to the end of this book. If you don't understand something, treat it like a manual and you can come back to it time and time again. Do not just put it back on the shelf and treat the ideas as something you may think about… Try it, take a look at your offers and go and have some more conversations. At the beginning of this book you were asked a very simple question, how many conversations did you have last week? To close, there's just a very simple question…

From the Authors

How many questions are you going to have next week?

Both Brad & I wish you all of the best with your businesses. It makes us immensely happy knowing that you are going to use the ideas in this book to drive more growth, better service, and create an overall better business environment for you, your customers and your team. Please tell us how you get on and if there is anything missing from this book, shout about it. There is more to come, we can't just leave you at your conversation and we know that there is so much more to discuss. Focus now on what you have learned, getting raising hands and making your marketing predictable and consistent. From there, you will truly be on your way to having a business that is profitable and works without you.